Y0-CAF-140

A CENTURY IN THE MOUNTAINS

A CENTURY IN

CELEBRATING VERMONT'S LONG TRAIL

THE MOUNTAINS

EDITED BY TOM SLAYTON
FOREWORD BY BILL McKIBBEN

A CENTURY IN THE MOUNTAINS

Celebrating Vermont's Long Trail

Editor-in-Chief: Tom Slayton
Editors: Dave Blumenthal, Ruth Hare, Susan Shea, Val Stori
Design: Mason Singer, The Laughing Bear Associates
Copy Editor: Kate Mueller
Indexing: Reidun Dahle Nuquist
Photography/image consultant: David Goodman
Printing: Villanti & Sons, Printers

The Green Mountain Club, Inc.
4711 Waterbury-Stowe Road
Waterbury Center, VT 05677
802-244-7037
www.greenmountainclub.org

First Edition
2009
ISBN 978-1-888021-24-0

Previous spread:
Mount Mansfield summit ridge.

ACKNOWLEDGMENTS

This book represents the culmination of a process more than four years in length involving many members and leaders of the Green Mountain Club. The editors wish to thank all those who helped by contributing their time, professional expertise, anecdotes, photographs, and, above all, their enthusiasm and affection for the Green Mountain Club, the mountains themselves, and the Long Trail. Among them are:

Authors: Bill McKibben, Tom Slayton, Reidun Dahle Nuquist, Katy Klutznik, Laura Waterman, Bryan Pfeiffer, Charles W. Johnson, Val Stori, Susan Shea, Ben Rose.

Those who generously contributed photographs: Harris Abbott, Tom Anderson, Scot Applegate, Dave Blumenthal, Jamie Compos, Paul Houchens, Jen Karson, Matt Larson, Patrick Leahy, Dot Meyer and the Burlington Section, GMC, Mike Riddell, Ben Rose, Susan Shea, Clyde Smith, Val Stori, UVM Special Collections Dept., Jonathan Wahl, and Jeb Wallace-Brodeur.

Longtime GMC friends who shared their stories: Harris and Jan Abbott, Kate Walsh, Daan Zwick, Marge Fish, Heinz Trebitz, Don Whitney, Greg Western, Smith Edwards, Doris Washburn, Roderick Rice, Larry Nelson, Ted Vogt, Dave Wright.

Supporters of GMC history and archives projects: Dana Baron, Michael Chernick, Keri Foster, Jennifer Karson, Sylvia Plumb.

Will and Jane Curtis and Frank Lieberman for writing *Green Mountain Adventure, Vermont's Long Trail* for the Green Mountain Club's seventy-fifth anniversary.

Special thanks to Reidun Dahle Nuquist, Laura Waterman, and Publications Committee chair Steve Larose for inspiring and clarifying the concept of this book.

And all the volunteers.

THE LONG TRAIL

CONTENTS

Foreword
REMEMBERING WHO WE ARE
by Bill McKibben 9

1. THE LAY OF THE LAND
by Tom Slayton 13

2. A CENTURY OF CHANGE—AND GROWTH
by Reidun Dahle Nuquist 29

3. LIFE ON THE TRAIL, THEN AND NOW
by Tom Slayton 67

4. A TRAIL FOR ANY PACE
by Katy Klutznik 95

5. QUIET CONTEMPLATION—AND HARD WORK
by Val Stori 109

6. THE TRAILKEEPERS
by Val Stori 123

7. THE NATURAL WORLD
by Bryan Pfeiffer 141

8. TO MAKE IT LAST FOREVER
by Susan Shea 165

Afterword
THE TRAIL AHEAD
by Ben Rose 181

INDEX 188

FOREWORD

REMEMBERING WHO WE ARE

Mountains and Transformation

BY BILL McKIBBEN

I HAVE THE GREAT GOOD FORTUNE to live within a few miles' walk of the Long Trail. I can wander through the woods at my house, up an abandoned path, across the Forest Service trunk road, and hit the trail to Skylight Pond and the adjoining lodge in under two hours. If I've got a day to myself, I can cruise to Lincoln Gap or (long day) on to Mount Abe. Or turn south, up through the Middlebury ski bowl and deep into the Moosalamoo wilderness. I am lucky, and I'm smart enough to know I'm lucky.

But even on the days I don't get up high, the line of mountains is always there at my back, a constant reference, an unvarying beauty, a never-ending temptation and solace.

Fireweed enhances this view of the Green Mountains near Middlebury Gap.

That line of the Greens has always seemed special to me for many reasons. For one, it's the place where the East ends and the rest of America begins. It's the last bit of coastal geology, the north-south folds that derive from the crashing ocean plates. When you stand at their crest, you have New England at your back, and old England as well; you can imagine the salt snap of the ocean. Look west and the rest of America begins: the confused and glorious jumble of the Adirondacks, the Great Lakes beyond, the Great Plains beyond that.

But its hiking history, embodied in the Green Mountain Club, seems just as special. The idea that people would go take long hikes in the wilderness, which we think of as obvious, was not so clear when the club began.

The Sierra Club was in its infancy; the Appalachian Trail wasn't even a glimmer in the eye of Benton MacKaye. And yet the founders of this enterprise were correctly confident that it would find an enthusiastic membership.

Indeed it has. What pleasure to hike the Long Trail, not just for the twists and turns, the occasional views glimpsed through the trees, the spectacular summits, the moose, the tang of balsam crushed underfoot—but also for the people one encounters. The shelter stewards, hardy and lean after a month or two high up, always ready for some conversation; the old-timers, felt hats and Vibram soles and dual hiking poles; the college kids out for a weekend wander; best of all the families with young kids, doling out the M&Ms to keep short legs firing, building the next round of people who will keep this trail glorious for years to come.

In the fight to save the natural world—the whole world—from the environmental crises bearing down upon us, it's necessary to remember just how deeply important places like the Long Trail really are. Not just for relaxation, not just for recreation, not just for scenery—but for allowing us to remember who we are. Allowing us to feel small again in the face of the large forces of wind and weather. Allowing us to feel young, and properly insignificant, in the face of ancient granite and massive shaggy yellow birch. Allowing us to feel cold and hot and tired and hungry and all the other things that modern life normally keeps at bay—and so allowing us to feel warm around a campfire and rested in a sleeping bag and happily filled with the kind of dinner you can cook on a WhisperLite. And so, in turn, putting in some reasonable perspective the consumer world we normally inhabit.

There's scarcely an environmentalist I've ever known who didn't have some kind of deep experience, usually early on, in the largeness of the outdoor world. Who didn't have some epiphany under the stars or the moon or the late autumn rain of yellow leaves. They took those peak experiences back down the mountain with them and used them as the fuel to fire the writing, the chart compiling, the lobbying, the legislating, the fund-raising—all the work that has helped maintain the world we have been called to steward. Work like that has maintained the Long Trail all these years—but the Long Trail has helped maintain the larger work of Vermont environmentalists, given us a place to remember why we're fighting and what the stakes really are.

A year ago, our local junior high, the North Branch School, decided on a three-day spring hike along the Long Trail, working south from Lincoln Gap. The snow was gone down here in the village, and the mountains no longer wore their winter coat of rime. But when the kids got there, they quickly found that winter lingered along the trail in the form of three feet of snow. They post-holed for those three days, slowly up and down the paths that are steep enough even at the height of summer. It was, by every account, hard work. It was also, by every account, pure glory. They learned they could do something hard, they learned their backyard held deep adventure, they learned that the strong needed to help the tired. They emerged carrying a moose rack they'd found up high and carrying a new sense of themselves.

How often has that story been repeated along the Long Trail? Ten thousand times, I'd bet. And how often will it happen in the future? At least as often, or so I devoutly hope.

Opposite: On Camel's Hump summit.

THE MISSION OF THE GREEN MOUNTAIN CLUB is to make the Vermont mountains play a larger part in the life of the people by protecting and maintaining the Long Trail System and fostering, through education, the stewardship of Vermont's hiking trails and mountains.

CHAPTER 1

THE LAY OF THE LAND

The Long Trail and the Green Mountain Club

BY TOM SLAYTON

VERMONT'S GREEN MOUNTAINS are as linear as a plow's turned furrow. Unlike other mountains of the Northeast, they lie in an extended north-south range more than 250 miles long. So in retrospect, it is easy to understand why James Paddock Taylor, headmaster, outdoorsman, and civic booster, on a rainy hike near Stratton Mountain in 1909, conceived the idea of a single trail, a Long Trail, traversing the entire range.

The idea of a long-distance hiking trail along a single mountain range was new to Vermont, and new to America at the time. No such trail had ever been built before. But the times — and the shape of the mountains themselves — demanded it. It now seems almost inevitable.

From Hunger Mountain in the Worcester range, looking southwest across White Rocks, the linear nature of the main range of the Green Mountains can be seen clearly.

What was not inevitable and could not have been foreseen was the way the resulting Long Trail changed the mountains and how the club that built it participated in and shaped the changes that came to the state of Vermont over the next century. Those changes encompassed the greatest social and technological transformation in Vermont's history. From a quiet, economically depressed, rural backwater, the state was transformed into a vigorous, distinctive part of contemporary America — fast-forwarded into the modern world. And the Long Trail was an important part of it all.

The Green Mountain Club (GMC) was formed in 1910 "to make the Vermont mountains play a larger part in the life of the people." More specifically, the club was created with a job to do: to build Taylor's master trail, linking Vermont's mountains in an unbroken line from Massachusetts to Canada. It took twenty years, but the club succeeded in both its tough particular task and its lofty overarching goal. The trail was built, and sure enough, more Vermonters began to discover and celebrate their mountains.

GMC founder James P. Taylor on a winter hike in 1928.

By popularizing mountain recreation in Vermont, the GMC and the Long Trail played a significant role in the state's twentieth-century transformation into a small, but distinctive rural entity with an independent streak and a strong environmental conscience.

None of those changes could have been predicted, nor could founders of the club have known in 1910 that the GMC itself would be transformed in the century ahead. What began as a club focused on trail building and maintenance became, over the years, a wide-ranging organization with a strong (though subtly expressed) environmental mission, a knack for low-key outdoor education, and the management responsibility for a corridor of protected land that surrounds the Long Trail along the Green Mountain ridgeline.

VERMONT'S GREEN MOUNTAINS

The Green Mountains themselves, once thought of as little more than an inconvenient barrier between eastern and western Vermont, are now recognized as a unique and fascinating resource — economic, recreational, ecological, and spiritual. They are amply supplied with places of grandeur and deep natural beauty.

Opposite: Austin Brook descends through fall color in the Breadloaf Wilderness Area, Green Mountain National Forest.

The Long Trail, which follows the crest of the long north-south range, is gentler in its southern sections, roughly from the Massachusetts border to its midpoint near Sherburne Pass. In the south, the trail traverses great unbroken forests that cloak the sprawling ridges of Glastenbury Mountain and the picturesque summit of Stratton Mountain and nearby Stratton Pond. Little Rock Pond, a beautiful mountain lake with a tiny, rocky islet, lies not far south of White Rocks Cliffs, where deeply faulted rocks, shattered by the actions of frost and thaw, have piled boulders and talus in immense, cascading heaps that are visible for miles. Near Rutland, the trail climbs over the rugged range that rises from Shrewsbury quickly to the rocky

A quiet morning at Stratton Pond. Opposite: Some Long Trail signs have been around for a while.

summit of Killington, second-highest peak in Vermont. Just north of that point, the Appalachian Trail, which shares the Long Trail's route northward from Massachusetts, branches off toward the east, bound for New Hampshire and Maine.

The northern half of the Green Mountain range is generally higher and more rugged than the southern half. Outstanding peaks like Camel's Hump, Mount Abraham, Mount Mansfield, and Jay Peak thrust their rocky shoulders above tree line, and from the Winooski River south to Middlebury Gap, a high ridgetop portion of the Long Trail known as the Monroe Skyline winds over rocky outcrops and through wooded glens, offering a striking array of mountain scenery.

Mount Mansfield, the highest summit in Vermont, lifts a great rocky spine above tree line with a commanding presence, broad views, and the most extensive alpine meadow in Vermont, stretching along its summit for more than a mile. Although it has been the locus of mountaintop development for more than a century — a ridgetop hotel and carriage road in the nineteenth century, communications towers and a major ski area in the twentieth — most of the mountain's main ridgeline is now protected. It is a refuge for rare plants and birds and an exhilarating walk for hikers.

The mountain that may be the closest to the hearts of Vermonters is Camel's Hump, the distinctive, rock-capped peak that rises abruptly south of the Winooski River. It is the highest undeveloped mountain in Vermont, the only 4,000-foot peak without ski trails on its flanks or communications towers on its summit. The eccentric nineteenth-century millionaire Joseph Battell of Middlebury bought the mountain and surrounding land and gave it to the state of Vermont in 1911. Despite sporadic attempts to open it to development, it has been protected since then and is recognized today as a natural treasure that appears on the state quarter-dollar and (along with Mount Mansfield) on the state coat of arms.

Both mountains are spectacular, but where Mansfield is grand, expansive, and open, Camel's Hump is subtle, less spectacular, and wilder. The view from the summit is an unparalleled 360-degree

Hiker crossing Burnt Rock Mountain in winter.

Trailside ferns.

Opposite: Long Trail on Camel's Hump, north of Montclair Glen.

panorama that on clear days reaches west across Lake Champlain to the Adirondacks, east to the White Mountains in New Hampshire, north to Mansfield's rocky spine and beyond, and as far south as Killington and Ascutney.

Yet closer at hand, the view from Camel's Hump, like views from other peaks in the Green Mountains, is of pastoral valleys, farmed and inhabited by people. This is, in fact, one of the distinguishing characteristics of the Green Mountains — a function, again, of their long, narrow conformation: they are close to the places where Vermonters live and work. They are intimate, friendly mountains and have long been companions to the life lived in the valleys below them. In that, they are different from the wilder, more forbidding mountains of upstate New York, New Hampshire, and Maine.

By building the Long Trail along the length of the Green Mountains in the two decades between 1910 and 1930, the GMC made Vermont's mountains more accessible to all Vermonters and opened their broad views and secret places to those willing to walk the trail. There must be thousands of spots — wooded glens filled with ferns, meadows rich with wildflowers, mysterious, fertile bogs, narrow, rocky defiles and notches — that would have gone forever unnoticed had the Long Trail never been built. What a letter writer to the *Burlington Free Press* wrote in 1919 still holds true today:

"There were ledges one-half mile long and as the trail wound round these, all sorts of fairy caverns came into view. It gave us a feeling that fairies, imps, and gnomes scampered to cover just in time to hide from us."

That section of the Long Trail, over the Stark Mountains, maintains its rugged, mysterious character and can evoke much the same feeling from hikers today. And there are many other such places. The Long Trail remains one of the most beautiful and interesting hiking trails in the Northeast and one of Vermont's indisputable cultural and natural treasures.

Love of Vermont's mountains started the GMC and has kept it vigorous through the years. Top: Near Stratton Mountain in 1921. Bottom: Long Trail Patrol, 1977.

Opposite: Contemporary hikers replenish their water supply at Stratton Pond.

THE CLUB THAT BUILT THE TRAIL

For a century, the organization that has maintained the trail and protected the mountaintops has been the GMC. The club was formed in 1910 specifically to clear and construct the trail. (The appropriateness of the term *construct* becomes evident only after you have watched the strong, young members of the Long Trail Patrol move literally tons of rock, tree roots, gravel, and mud to reconstruct some ailing section of the trail. Trail building is work.)

As mentioned above, it took the GMC some twenty years to build the Long Trail completely from Massachusetts to Canada. Almost immediately upon its completion, the club began to change and its mission began to expand.

Beginning with the "Green Mountain Parkway" fight of the 1930s, the GMC had to go beyond trail building and maintenance and become an advocacy organization. Since then it has, of necessity, become the leading environmental steward of the main range of the Green Mountains and the trail that traverses it. That transformation is all the more remarkable because James P. Taylor, the club's founder, was not an environmentalist—at all. He was a schoolteacher and principal who morphed into a chamber-of-commerce-oriented civic booster.

Nevertheless, the club's transformation did occur, driven by the social and environmental changes embodied in a changing Vermont and by the abiding love that members of the club had—and have—for the Green Mountains.

The club's history will be more completely told in chapter 2. But for the time being, it should be pointed out that the growth and change in the GMC's mission came about because the club chose to respond to several major threats to the integrity of the Long Trail and the Green Mountains. The most significant of those threats were:

1. The proposed Green Mountain Parkway in the mid-1930s.
2. The hiking boom of the 1960s and early 1970s.
3. Shifts in property ownership along the main range of the Green Mountains in the 1980s and the resulting growth of high-altitude mountain development, both commercial and residential.

Fireweed blossoms.

Opposite: A gallery of Rutland County hiking images: evening at Governor Clement Shelter; two views of Clarendon Gorge bridge; trail signs and trail friendship; an assortment of footwear.

The Green Mountain Parkway was proposed in 1933 as a high-altitude highway, running the length of the Green Mountains, much like the Blue Ridge Parkway in Virginia. Although Taylor, the club's visionary founder, enthusiastically favored the parkway, the membership opposed it and fought successfully to defeat it. The struggle was a defining moment for the GMC. In it, the club played a crucial role in defeating the parkway and established itself as a pro-environmental voice for the mountains.

The next major challenge came, ironically, from forces released by the club and the Long Trail itself. In the 1960s and 1970s, a surge in the popularity of hiking threatened to overwhelm the Long Trail system. Suddenly, more than 150,000 people per year were walking at least some part of the trail; favorite summits and shelters began to be blighted by overuse. The club responded with hiker-education programs and hired summit caretakers to protect fragile alpine summits. Those programs continue today, a part of the GMC's expanded role as mountain caretaker.

The growing pressure of high-altitude mountain development in the 1980s confronted the club with its most serious threat. Ownership patterns were changing, and it began to seem that much of the Long Trail might be compromised by ski areas, condominium developments, even large private homes high in the mountains. And so, according to GMC executive director Ben Rose, "There was an epiphany among the club directors that if we wanted to have the trail continue, we had better buy it."

Over the ensuing decade, the club became "a high-elevation land trust," Rose says. It raised the roughly $9 million needed to protect the Long Trail—essentially by establishing a protected strip of land along the top of the northern Green Mountains. (Most of the southern and central portions of the Long Trail were already rendered development-free by the Green Mountain National Forest.)

AT/LT SOUTH

AT/LT NORTH

S
LONG TRAIL
N
BOYCE SHELTER
MIDDLEBURY GAP
BURNT HILL TRAIL

APPALACHIAN TRAIL NORTH
SHERBURNE PASS 1.4 MI
GIFFORD WOODS (VT 100) 2.1 MI
KATAHDIN 469 MI

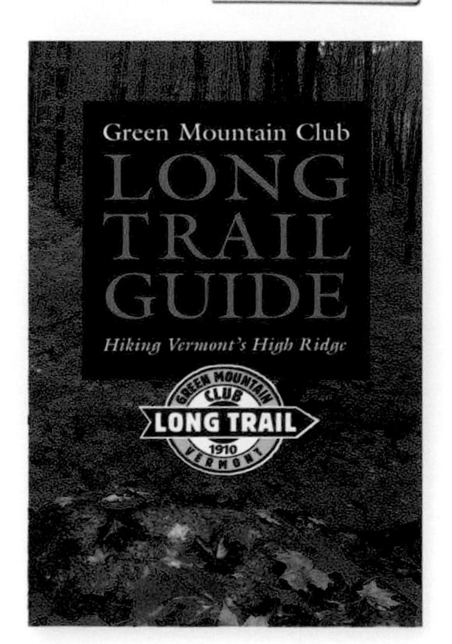

By the time the GMC's one hundredth birthday approached, it had grown from the original 23 stalwarts to an organization with almost 10,000 members, 10 full-time employees (plus another 50 trail workers and caretakers during hiking season), and a broad range of activities and responsibilities. There were classes and workshops in subjects ranging from backwoods first aid to trail construction to orienteering with map and compass. A publications program produced trail guides, maps, a quarterly magazine, and more. A cadre of summer caretakers watched over every major summit and the most heavily used shelters. A small staff of paid workers and a much larger force of willing volunteers did trail work, repaired and rebuilt shelters, and sometimes even constructed new ones.

Because the club had come to own a significant amount of mountain land and easements, stewardship activities — inspection, boundary surveys, and the like — became an important part of its work. And the necessary administrative activities of any large organization had also expanded, requiring an administrative staff.

AN INFORMAL, EFFECTIVE STYLE

What sort of organization had evolved to fulfill all these responsibilities? Though transformed in many ways, the twenty-first-century GMC is still recognizable as the sprightly descendant of the small group that first assembled in 1910.

The club was — and is — informal, highly collaborative, friendly, somewhat resistant to change, and consistently antiauthoritarian. An anecdote related by Executive Director Rose is illustrative:

He was working one Saturday with a group of volunteers, building a new shelter on Bamforth Ridge, north of Camel's Hump. Most of the work was pure grunt labor, and that's what Rose was doing, carrying two-by-eights. Someone else was measuring and sawing, and other people were hammering down floorboards, raising wall forms, and so on. Someone new on the site asked Rose who was in charge.

"I looked around and thought, 'Well, I am the executive director...,'" Rose recalled. "Then I saw the president of the club, Andrew Nuquist, working nearby, the head of the Montpelier Section, Bill Clark, and a couple of other people who happened to be very skilled carpenters and builders . . . and I realized I had no idea who was in charge!"

The cliffy south face of Camel's Hump looms high above the approaching Long Trail.

Opposite: Guidebooks have evolved through the years, both typographically and in overall format.

Probably no one else on the job site that day did either. But the shelter got built anyway. That's just the way it is in the Green Mountain Club.

Volunteering is practically part of the club's DNA—a vital characteristic, given the amount of maintenance and repair that the trail and shelters regularly require. "The amount of work it takes to keep the trail in shape is stupendous," says former club president Andrew Nuquist. "Fortunately, the club is a passion for many people—people are devoted to it."

STEWARD OF THE GREEN MOUNTAINS

The GMC has avoided partisan politics throughout its history, rising to public advocacy only when its namesake mountains have been threatened. And so the club has avoided taking public positions on such matters as global warming and acid rain, assuming that its role is not to solve the larger environmental problems of the world but to focus closely on its local mission. "So far, the club has done a pretty good job of staying out of the really divisive environmental issues," Nuquist says.

The organization's deep devotion to the mountains and the Long Trail has placed it athwart the thrust of mainstream society on more than one occasion. It has been an inherently conservative force in Vermont's landscape, resisting significant change in the mountains whenever possible. In that way, the club goes against the grain of American society, and presents Executive Director Rose with an interesting built-in management challenge:

"How do you manage for stasis," he asks, "in a society that promotes growth?"

Even so, the Green Mountain Club remains one of the best-known and most widely respected organizations in Vermont. About half of the $9 million raised by the club to buy land and easements to protect the trail came from the Vermont Legislature, because of the club's long-term role, which the legislature defined in a resolution honoring the club "as founder, sponsor, and defender of the Long Trail."

Much of the public's approval of the GMC's work is doubtless due to the immense public service it provides — a free hiking trail through beautiful forests, across some of the most striking mountains in the Northeast. The club's long history and broad membership base also help. But there is a deeper reason: In maintaining the beauty and integrity of Vermont's mountain lands, the GMC is providing a framework for great adventures and a continuing connection to wild nature.

"It gives people a reason to feel alive," Rose notes. "It's really one of the higher expressions of humanity to want something like the Long Trail."

From the Stratton Mountain fire tower, Somerset Reservoir sparkles in the distance.

KILLINGTON 82 M.
MASSACHUSETTS
STATE LINE 181.6
CAMELS HUMP 4.5 M
MONTCLAIR GLEN 6.5 M
LINCOLN MT. 25.8
A FOOTPATH IN THE WILDERNESS
LONG TRAIL
DUNSMOOR LODGE 5.6 M
SUMMIT BOLTON MT. 6.7 M
LAKE MANSFIELD 9.8 M
SUMMIT 15.4 M
MT. MANSFIELD
TAFT LODGE 17.2 M
G M C

CHAPTER 2

A CENTURY OF CHANGE—AND GROWTH

A Short History of the GMC

BY REIDUN DAHLE NUQUIST

FEW OF THE MANY THOUSANDS of people who hike the Long Trail realize that it is the oldest long-distance hiking trail in the United States and that it predates the more renowned Appalachian Trail, which it inspired.

The Long Trail also precedes the establishment of most state parks and forests, the Green Mountain National Forest, ski resorts and touring centers, the Catamount Trail, which it also motivated, and today's bike paths and snowmobile trails. You could be forgiven for calling the Long Trail Vermont's oldest designated recreation resource.

In this hand-colored glass slide image by Theron Dean, two young hikers stop for a snack at a GMC trail sign, near the Winooski River in Bolton.

It is likely that even fewer people connect the trail to the Green Mountain Club (GMC), although without the GMC there would be no Long Trail: the club was founded a century ago with the specific purpose of building the trail. It is difficult to say which came first, the concept of the Long Trail or the GMC.

The Green Mountains dominate the Vermont landscape in a way that the more remote Adirondacks of New York and the White Mountains of New Hampshire do not. Vermont's mountains and foothills are constantly on the horizon, as recognizable to the inhabitants of the Champlain and Connecticut River Valleys as they are to those who live among them. Yet, the

Vermonters who founded the GMC in 1910 wanted the mountains to be more than a scenic backdrop: They wanted the mountains to play a larger part in people's lives.

In the nineteenth century, Vermont had seen well-heeled travelers bypass the Green Mountains for the higher, wilder peaks of its neighbor states. Vacationers sought an esthetic experience as much as peaks to climb — just being among mountains was appealing to those who lived in urban areas.

The reality: Hiking in the early days of the Long Trail could be a rugged, sweaty business, as these trail-clearers knew.

Laura and Guy Waterman, in their encyclopedic *Forest and Crag: A History of Hiking, Trail Blazing, and Adventure in the Northeast Mountains* (1989, 2003), describe how tourists — and Vermonters — gradually grew to appreciate the Green Mountains. This newfound interest in the Vermont landscape coincided with the growth of an emerging middle class with leisure time and disposable income. An extensive railroad network made the state accessible, as did the growing number of privately owned automobiles and an expanding highway system.

As the twentieth century dawned, accommodations expanded as well. Vermonters opened their homes to visitors, and local entrepreneurs added new lodgings to already existing hotels, summit houses, and mountain huts. In the century's first decade, the Ascutney Mountain Association (1903) and the Camel's Hump Club (1908) counted hundreds of climbers annually.

The first Vermont mountain climbers — Native Americans as well as early New England settlers — had, of course, bushwhacked their way up many peaks. So did the eminent walker Alden Partridge (1785–1854), founder of Norwich Academy (now Norwich University), who once covered thirty-four miles in one day and frequently brought his cadets along on multiday tramps.

With the number of tourists growing, enterprising hotel owners built carriage roads and bridle paths up Ascutney, Pisgah, Burke, Camel's Hump, Equinox, Mansfield, Hunger, Killington, Snake, and Lincoln mountains. Traces of these roads are still visible today. As recreational walking took off, footpaths gradually developed on the most popular mountains. But a trail network was still lacking.

The romance: However, hiking was a fashionable pursuit in the formative years of the GMC, and was often promoted with romantic images such as this one, taken at the hut clearing on Camel's Hump.

THE FOUNDING OF THE GREEN MOUNTAIN CLUB

According to GMC lore, the Long Trail was conceived by James P. Taylor one rainy July day in 1909, as he sat in his open tent staring at nearby "misty Stratton," a mountain practically unreachable because of a lack of trails. This is the story Taylor himself told. However, the genesis of the Long Trail is a bit more complex.

It so happened that 1909 was also the year of the Champlain Tercentennial—the three hundredth anniversary of Samuel de Champlain's arrival on the lake that bears his name. On July 8, as part of a weeklong celebration, fifty thousand people descended on Burlington to see and hear President William Howard Taft and other dignitaries in City Hall Park. One of them, British ambassador James Bryce, world traveler and mountain climber, predicted that in Vermont there would be an "increasing longing among the people to enjoy the scenic loveliness of this land of lakes and mountains." He counseled Vermonters "to keep open the mountains, and allow no one to debar pedestrians from climbing to their tops and wandering along their slopes. . . ." State newspapers printed his remarks in full.

Trail signs point the way.

Less than a year later, on March 11, 1910, at two o'clock, twenty-three Vermonters met in the Sample Room of the Van Ness House, across from City Hall Park, to form the GMC. They had been called together by Taylor to hear his plans for a single trail, linking the highest peaks of the Green Mountains.

The club's founders, all invited, were community leaders. They included school superintendents, lawyers, editors, journalists, a judge, a minister, and a college professor. Letters of regret came from Governor George H. Prouty and Joseph A. DeBoer, president of National Life Insurance Company. Both soon joined the club, as did former governors Urban A. Woodbury and Fletcher D. Proctor and U.S. Senators Carroll S. Page and William P. Dillingham.

Given the founders' backgrounds, it is no surprise that they gave the GMC a solid organizational framework, including local sections, or chapters, which has served the club well to this day. With its single-minded goal of making "the Vermont mountains play a larger part in the life of the people"—still its mission today—the GMC became, in the words of the Watermans, the country's "first true trail club, as distinct from a hiking or all-purpose outdoor club," like its older Boston-based cousin, the Appalachian Mountain Club (1876).

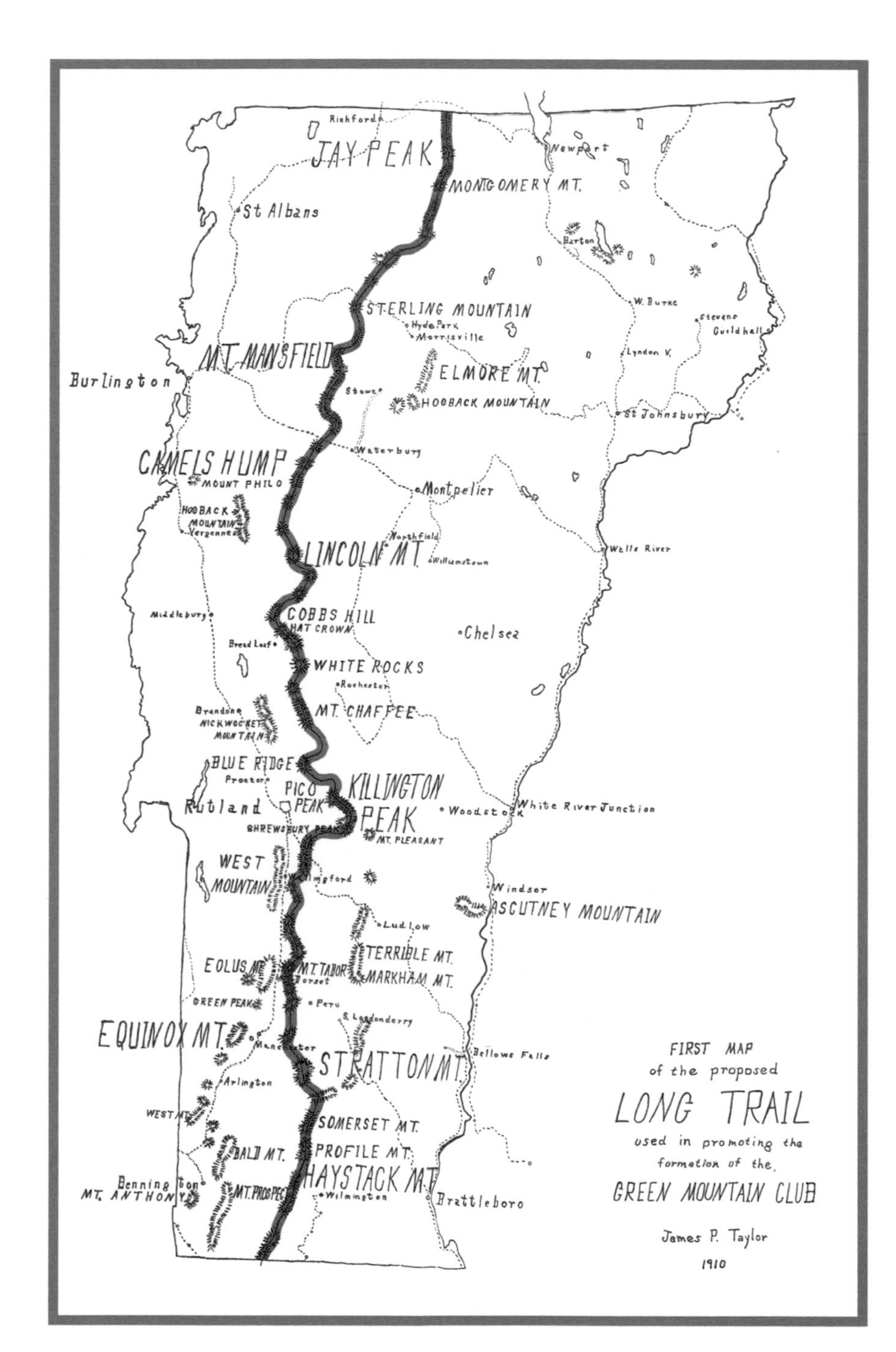

Above: These fashionably dressed 1920 hikers are happy to have reached the summit of Lincoln Mountain.

Left: The Long Trail as a concept: James P. Taylor's original 1910 map, which he used to promote the trail.

A board of fourteen councilors (later called trustees, now directors) representing Vermont's fourteen counties, governed the organization. Its first officers were James P. Taylor of Saxtons River, president; Judge Seneca Haselton of Burlington, vice president; E. L. Ingalls of Hartford, secretary; and C. W. Brownell of Burlington, treasurer.

JAMES P. TAYLOR

We don't know if Taylor was present at the Champlain Tercentennial celebration in Burlington, but he probably had read or heard of Ambassador Bryce's admonition to Vermonters to keep the mountains open to "pedestrians." (Subsequent correspondence between Bryce and Louis J. Paris, GMC membership chairman, credits the ambassador with inspiring the club's formation.) Be that as it may, the Green Mountains were receiving new attention, and the idea of promoting the mountains as a place for recreation was widespread. Vermont was receptive to an organization that would build trails and promote walking, and James P. Taylor was the man who acted on the idea.

James P. Taylor (above) in his later years. The photo was taken circa 1947.

Opposite, top: Hikers atop Mount Abraham in 1916 strike a variety of poses, from intrepid to exhausted.

Bottom: The Burlington Section on a hike to Taylor Lodge on Washington's Birthday, February 22, 1927. Fifth from left, front row, is GMC founder James P. Taylor.

James Paddock Taylor (1872–1949) came to Vermont in 1908 to be assistant principal at Vermont Academy in Saxtons River. A New Yorker, he attended Colgate University and did graduate work at Harvard and Columbia before joining Vermont Academy, a preparatory school with emphasis on "life in the open."

The young educator started an outing club and, like Alden Partridge before him, brought his students into the "Grand Campus" that was Vermont. The lack of trails and lodgings, however, led to "a year of mountain comedies and mountain tragedies." On one hike, the students nearly missed the view from Prospect Rock, near Manchester, because of a poorly penciled sign. On Killington Peak, porcupines kept them awake all night by gnawing on the ramshackle summit house and, adding insult to injury, upended the pot of fresh asparagus that was set aside for breakfast. Taylor looked in vain to the Appalachian Mountain Club (AMC) for assistance with trail building, but the Appies thought Vermont too flat to be of interest. As Taylor later wrote in *Footpath in the Wilderness: The Long Trail in the Green Mountains of Vermont* (1941), if "a mountain trail system were to be constructed in the Green Mountains, Vermonters would have to build it."

Taylor drew a map with a line up and down the Green Mountain range and spent the rest of 1909 promoting his idea of a long trail that would connect existing hiking trails. He talked to anyone who would listen, including the governor and state forester. Having to step in for his principal at a banquet for Vermont schoolmasters, he spent half his allotted time describing his trail proposal to the state's top educators, several of whom became GMC charter members.

A typical camp in the early years of the GMC, tent pitched and supper cooking on an open fire. This photo was taken in 1919 in Cooley Glen.

Two pioneer members of the Bennington Section, Irving Hare (left) and Willis White, pose in Hagar Clearing in 1916.

THE FIRST MILES

The idea of the Long Trail was introduced; now it was up to members of the fledgling GMC to make it reality. They began with the thirty-mile segment from Mount Mansfield to Camel's Hump. Taylor spent his 1910 vacation scouting the route. He soon proved to be more of a pied piper than a trail builder, however, preferring to schmooze with landowners to obtain permission for the trail to cross their property. Fortunately, other members stepped into the breach and began the actual construction of the trail.

That fall and the following spring, attorney Clarence P. Cowles of the Mount Mansfield (now Burlington) Section, the club's oldest, and Craig O. Burt of Stowe blazed and cut the trail from Mansfield's summit to Nebraska Notch. At the end of the day, Burt had a relatively short hike home to Stowe, while Cowles had to trek to Underhill to catch the Burlington trolley.

These lads take in the view from Dean Panorama near Stark Mountain. The spot was one of many named by the indefatigable Will Monroe, who built much of the Long Trail in this section. To the north, Camel's Hump defines the horizon.

By the end of the second year, the two had cleared a trail from Smugglers' Notch over Mansfield and Bolton to the Winooski River. Judge Cowles is the second key figure in the early history of the GMC: he built additional trails on Mount Mansfield and supervised the construction of Taft Lodge (1920). Cowles died in 1963, at age eighty-seven, while snowshoeing to Wiley Lodge on the northern flank of Camel's Hump with the Burlington Section.

James Taylor understood the promotional value of first completing the scenic Mount Mansfield–Camel's Hump segment. He enlisted the support of Charles R. Cummings, editor of *The Vermonter*, and in May 1911, the magazine published a special mountain issue. In describing the Long Trail, it reported that "The Winooski River at Bolton is ferried by boat, adding a picturesque interest to the jaunt." With help from the newly formed Vermont Bureau of Publicity, the club bought 5,000 copies, 3,000 of which were mailed out-of-state. (Between 1911 and 1913, *The Vermonter* ran a regular column of "Green Mountain Club Notes," serving as the club's first newsletter.)

Carefully crafted stone steps make the ascent easier.

During the wet summer of 1912, the Long Trail expanded only from Smugglers' Notch north to Sterling Pond. Taylor, knowing the trail needed more workers and money than the Burlington Section alone could provide, concentrated on organizing new sections, and Bread Loaf, Brandon, Rutland, Sterling, and Bennington Sections were born. The Camel's Hump Club soon joined the effort.

Taylor also approached Austin F. Hawes, Vermont's first state forester and himself a walker, for help. Hawes needed a fire-patrol trail south of Camel's Hump and thought it might double as a hiking trail. If the GMC could pay for construction, the Forestry Department would build the trail. According to Jane and Will Curtis and Frank Lieberman in their *Green Mountain Adventure: Vermont's Long Trail* (1985), the GMC raised $1,065 for labor. When money ran out, the AMC kindly came to the rescue. By August 1913, the Long Trail reached south to Killington Peak. That same year, the Bennington Section cleared trail from the Massachusetts line to Stratton Mountain and the Sterling Section from Sterling Pond to Johnson. The trail was now almost 150 miles long.

Satisfaction was short lived. Hikers reported that the trail was hard to follow, and they were getting lost. Worse, the low-lying, 15 percent grade corridor that the foresters had so swiftly cut to enable them to bring fire-fighting equipment up the wooded slopes missed

Opposite, top: Trail clearing party with Will Monroe (second from right) on Romance Mountain. Note the sporty bandannas, and the presence of women trail workers.

Bottom: These men are resting after having notched the large logs in the foreground, which will become the sills to the original Sucker Brook Lodge, south of Middlebury Gap.

Cooking *al fresco* at Griffith Lake Shelter in 1936.

most outlooks. This was not the scenic Long Trail the club's founders had envisioned! Supporters of the state forester argued that it was a reasonable trail that the average person could follow.

Taylor, perhaps disheartened, began withdrawing from what had for him become "the long trial." In 1912, he had left Vermont Academy to become executive secretary of the Greater Vermont Association, later the Vermont Chamber of Commerce. The GMC was languishing; only the dedicated Louis Paris kept the organization from unraveling. Then in 1914, the Great War broke out in Europe.

Opposite: Camel's Hump rises majestically above Wind Gap on a cloudy day.

Will Monroe, fiery and determined, helped make the Long Trail both beautiful and challenging by routing it over the highest summits and most scenic spots in the central Green Mountains. He is shown (left) with five of his beloved dogs in 1928 and (above) in his trademark bandanna, painting a trail blaze.

THE MONROE SKYLINE

The war brought professor Will Monroe to Vermont in 1914. He was the last of the troika of Long Trail giants—and the most eccentric. He had been wont to spend summers climbing in Europe. Now he signed up to teach summer school at the University of Vermont, eager to investigate local hiking opportunities. He was not impressed with the graded Long Trail/fire patrol trail.

Will S. Monroe (1863–1939), born in Pennsylvania and educated at Stanford University and in Europe, was something of a renaissance man. Head of the psychology department at the New Jersey State Normal School at Montclair, he was passionate about education, the poetry of Walt Whitman, dogs, gastronomy, botany, and walking. Now he became passionate about improving the Long Trail and elevating it "from one that was merely long to one that was a classic for beauty and interest."

George Mathers contemplates his supper at Hell Hollow Camp near Bennington, circa 1916. Not every trail meal was an unalloyed delight.

With a nod from the GMC leadership, in 1916 he went to work relocating it. With him came Louis Paris's son, Olden, and, from New Jersey, J. Ashton Allis and Dr. Kerson Nurian. Traveling by train, automobile, and finally by ox cart, they set up camp in what Monroe named Montclair Glen, below Camel's Hump. The professor and his crew picked their way south, blazing a route atop the ridges and incorporating as many scenic spots and lookouts as possible. With additional help from Judge Cowles and his good friend Theron S. Dean, also of Burlington, the crew cut 13.5 miles of new trail—all the way to Glen Ellen.

Back in New Jersey for the fall semester and full of enthusiasm for the Long Trail, Monroe organized friends and colleagues from New Jersey and New York into a new GMC section. The initiative was met with some skepticism back in Vermont, especially among members with ties to the Forestry Department. Nonetheless, the New York Section became the club's first out-of-state chapter, with Monroe as president. It was long one of the largest and most dynamic sections, until it severed its Vermont ties in 1999.

During 1917, Monroe and his Yorkers, with help from Cowles, Dean, and Olden Paris, cut their way to Lincoln Gap. With that, the Monroe Skyline from the Winooski River to Lincoln Gap—one of the most spectacular sections of the trail—was complete. That same year, Charles P. Cooper and Willis M. Ross, both of Rutland, scouted and built much of the trail from Killington south to Prospect Rock. Cooper's paint-spattered jacket became well known along the trail, as did the many signs he mounted at highway crossings.

Will Monroe in the spring of 1931, in professorial attire, with one of his dogs.

The Long Trail now stretched across the mountaintops from Johnson to Massachusetts. The GMC marked the achievement by issuing the first Long Trail guidebook, a modest fifty-cent pamphlet that included the names of all seven hundred members. It described the trail and its earliest overnight facilities, none of which resembled the large, staffed AMC huts in the White Mountains. The GMC shelters and camps were simple huts or three-sided log shelters, spaced about a day's walk apart. Where no accommodations were available, hikers approached nearby farms for lodging and fresh provisions.

Hikers meant extra income not just for local farm families but also for those directly engaged in the tourist industry: innkeepers; café, store, and gas station owners; bus companies and railroads. As the popularity of the Long Trail grew, the Vermont Bureau of Publicity used it to promote the Green Mountains outside the state. Lodging directories stressed proximity to the Long Trail, and railroad annuals pointed out stops near trailheads. GMC leaders Louis Paris and Mortimer Proctor contributed to the travel literature, extolling the trail that wound "its snakelike course through the mountain fastnesses." *Vacation Tramps in New England Highlands* (1919), a popular book by Allen Chamberlain, Boston newspaperman and future president of the AMC, also helped make the Vermont trail known.

DOING AWAY WITH THE 'ALMOST'

In 1930, trail blazers (below, from left) Phillips D. Carleton and Charles G. Doll cut the Long Trail's last few miles from Jay Peak to the Canadian border.

With hikers flocking to the Long Trail, GMC trail builders were painfully aware that they had not reached their goal. In 1926, they at last extended the Long Trail north to Jay Peak or "almost to Canada." Another three years went by before brothers Bruce and Roy Buchanan declared "We better get rid of the almost" and blazed the remaining ten or so miles to Line Post 592 on the international border. Finally in 1930, Charles G. Doll and Phillips D. Carleton, both of the University of Vermont, followed the blazes and actually cut the remaining link.

It had taken twenty years to build the Long Trail envisioned by James Taylor. The result, then and today, is a rugged footpath where the hiker is constantly challenged by ups and downs, roots and rocks, where the rewards are solitude, birdsong, and rippling brooks, where unexpected rock outcroppings command inspired views of forest, sky, and mountains. It is Vermont's own backcountry trail, outlined on every state highway map and road atlas.

Though Vermont's mountains are not as high as neighboring peaks, the trail that traverses them is both beautiful and rugged. If you can hike the Long Trail, you are ready for most other trail adventures.

It remained for trail crews, like the one resting (right) at Line Post 592 on the Canadian border, to keep the trail open. Famed trail- and shelter-builder Roy Buchanan is seated, left.

TIME FOR CELEBRATION

The following year, the GMC could celebrate the completion of the Long Trail as well as its own coming of age, its twenty-first birthday. On September 12, 1931, three hundred people gathered at the Long Trail Lodge at Sherburne Pass for a grand party.

The lodge, the GMC's new official clubhouse, provided the perfect setting. Completed in 1923, it was a picturesque, rustic lodge designed by architect Paul W. Thayer. (He was also responsible for the stone Fay Fuller Camp, dedicated in 1930.) The interior framing was logs with the bark on. Boulders, with moss and ferns intact, were incorporated into the building. The white-blazed Long Trail, coming off Pico Peak, ran straight through the lodge. The furniture was what we today call Adirondack-style. Chandeliers and wall sconces were of birch limbs, and lamp shades of birch bark. James Taylor called the lodge — a gift of club president and future governor Mortimer R. Proctor and his mother — the "finest mountain camp in the world."

The interior of the Long Trail Lodge, which was built in 1923 and became GMC headquarters. Tragically, the lodge burned down in 1968.

The festivity began with speeches by Governor Stanley C. Wilson, Dorothy Canfield Fisher, Will Monroe, Taylor, and others. During dinner, served on the lodge's Wedgwood china, a male quartet entertained with song. At 9:15 P.M. a gong was struck twenty-one times — once for each year since the club's founding — a signal to light flares up and down the summits of the most prominent Green Mountains. They were seen from miles away.

The Long Trail Lodge was the scene of many club events, including annual meetings. It became a popular tourist destination, so popular, in fact, that the GMC finally had to opt out of the hospitality business, leasing it and adjacent buildings to a hotel corporation. Tragically, the lodge burned down in November 1968.

Opposite: Hiker near Mount Mansfield summit.

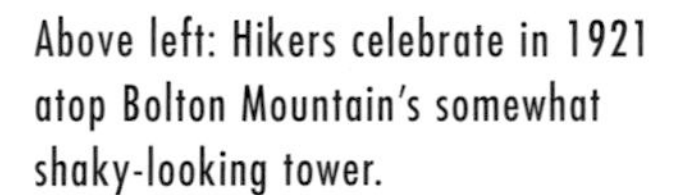

Above left: Hikers celebrate in 1921 atop Bolton Mountain's somewhat shaky-looking tower.

Right: During a trail-measuring excursion (note wheel), Herbert Wheaton Congdon rests at Dunsmoor Lodge on the flanks of Bolton Mountain.

MAINTAINING THE LONG TRAIL

While James P. Taylor may not have given much initial thought to maintaining the Long Trail, those who followed had no choice. The 1927 flood, the worst natural disaster in Vermont history, left the higher reaches of the Long Trail intact, but the highway crossing in Johnson and the club's ferry boat on the Winooski River disappeared, and the Bennington Section had to relocate a destroyed stretch near Webster Camp. Monroe, having retired two years earlier to his Couching Lion Farm in Duxbury, distributed $300 in donations from the New York Section among local flood victims, along with blankets from Long Trail lodges.

The great hurricane that slashed through Vermont on September 21, 1938, did extensive damage to the trail. The Burlington Section counted 252 downed trees between the Winooski River and Smugglers' Notch. Roy O. Buchanan of the Long Trail Patrol found similar havoc further north, including fifty blowdowns in one-half mile near Belvidere junction. The Killington Section had to relocate two miles of its part of the trail. In the days of only hand tools, repairing such widespread damage presented a major physical challenge.

Roy Buchanan, small but energetic, was beloved by many GMC members. He headed the Long Trail Patrol and was a key figure in establishing and maintaining the trail. Here, he shaves at the 1961 intersectional gathering at Plymouth.

The paid Long Trail Patrol, organized at the behest of club president Mortimer R. Proctor, did trail work where section volunteers were unavailable or where major construction was required. Buchanan, who taught electrical engineering at the University of Vermont, had joined the Long Trail Patrol in 1931, after assisting with the completion of the trail. He became its leader the following year, remaining with the patrol for thirty-six years until 1967, when Jack Harrington took over.

Just five feet two inches tall, Buchanan (1881–1977) claimed—probably correctly—that he could cut trail faster than most. But someone else had to follow, claimed his friend Daan Zwick, to "cut out the top branches so that a regular-sized fella could walk through." Buchanan helped build thirty-seven Long Trail lodgings, mostly in the north to fill in gaps. Many were enclosed camps of his own design: "large enough for six hikers or six porcupines, but not six hikers and six porcupines," as he put it. (Journey's End, one of the remaining Buchanan camps, was dismantled in 2006 and rebuilt on the GMC campus in Waterbury Center.)

Buchanan was a familiar figure along the trail. Almost as well known was his Patrol Truck No. 1, a Chevrolet pickup donated by Proctor, which Buchanan had furnished with bunks and a stove for himself and his young family. A warm and modest man, "Mr. Green Mountain Club" became a mentor to many young trail workers and was a popular presence at GMC gatherings. Buchanan Mountain in northern Vermont is named for him, as Bruce Peak is for his brother Bruce. Roy's sons, Chet and Andy, were other members of the remarkable Buchanan clan.

THE GREEN MOUNTAIN PARKWAY

In 1933, just three years after the Long Trail reached the Canadian border, a proposal for a scenic mountain parkway, modeled on Virginia's Skyline Drive, rocked the GMC. It was the decade of the Great Depression with unemployment, poverty, and bankruptcies. President Franklin D. Roosevelt launched his New Deal programs to help those in need. The Civilian Conservation Corps was particularly successful in Vermont, employing thousands of young men to build ski and hiking trails, state parks, and forest roads that are still in use today.

The Green Mountain Parkway was the idea of Colonel William J. Wilgus of Ascutney. He presented it as a federally funded project that would put Vermonters to work and, when completed, would bring needed tourist dollars to the state. His plan had the support of many prominent Vermonters, including Ralph Flanders, Dorothy Canfield Fisher, and Governor Stanley Wilson. Among the opponents were the novelist Sinclair Lewis, Vermont poet Walter Hard, and then governor George Aiken, who would later become senator from Vermont.

The Green Mountain Parkway, a major threat to the wilderness character of high ridges like these along the Long Trail, was rejected by Vermonters in 1936.

Opposite, top: In this early Theron Dean slide, Mount Mansfield is shown before it acquired ski trails and a national reputation. Note the open, farmed landscape of Stowe in the years before World War II.

Bottom: Most of the roads that gave access to the Long Trail in those days were unpaved. Here a group of hikers prepares to move out from Lincoln Gap. The photo was taken in 1935.

Reflecting the rift among Vermonters in general, many GMC members were in favor of the parkway, most prominent among them James P. Taylor and his friend Clarence Cowles. The board of trustees, however, was firmly against the idea. It quickly passed a resolution stating it was "unalterably opposed to the construction of such a highway," planned as it was to parallel and, at intervals, cross the Long Trail. It was argued that the highway would deface the landscape, attract the wrong sort of people, bring with it unwanted development, give the federal government too much control, and divide the state between east and west. Not to mention the cost to Vermont of acquiring the rights-of-way — money, they argued, that could be better spent repairing bridges and maintaining existing roads.

Those in favor claimed the Green Mountain Parkway was essential to the state's economic survival, that it would make Vermont's mountains accessible to all, and that it would bring together the two sides of the state. Taylor, by then representing the Vermont Chamber of Commerce and a champion of road beautification, saw the parkway as progress needed to bring Vermont into the twentieth century.

The intense public debate over the Green Mountain Parkway raged for three years. Historian Blake Harrison, in *The View from Vermont: Tourism and the Making of an American Rural Landscape* (2006),

LONG
A FOOTPATH IN
TRAIL
THE WILDERNESS
56·900

In 1935, the summit ridge of Mount Mansfield had no communications towers. The Green Mountain Parkway, which would have compromised the ridge, was on its way to being defeated in a 1936 statewide referendum. This photo looks northward from the Forehead toward the Nose and the summit ridge.

calls it the first statewide battle over "balancing growth and scenic beauty." The parkway's final defeat came in a 1936 town meeting day referendum where it lost by twelve thousand votes. The GMC leadership, having waged a tireless campaign against it, could claim much of the credit. (A second parkway proposal surfaced and was rejected in 1965. As a compromise, Route 100 was designated a scenic road.)

The remainder of the decade was relatively quiet for the GMC. The Great Depression took its toll on membership dues. Observing the rising popularity of skiing in Vermont, the club appointed a committee on winter sports and promoted the Long Trail Lodge at Sherburne Pass to those coming north on weekend ski trains from Boston and New York. Cleared corduroy roads around the lodge provided "easy gradual slopes for novices," and a half-mile track brought guests to the ski tow at Pico Peak. Daily rates at the lodge's new winter annex were three to four dollars on the American plan.

Then came World War II.

WORLD WAR II

Many GMC members went off to war while others worked long days at home for the war effort. Few had the time, money, or the inclination to go hiking. Gasoline for private use was difficult to come by, and buses and trains were crowded. The Long Trail Patrol was dissolved for the duration, and the trail was, of necessity, neglected. Louis B. Puffer, Long Trail guidebook editor and cartographer, advised hikers to "blame Hitler or Hirohito instead of the Green Mountain Club" for poor trail conditions.

Army private—and future club president—Arthur R. Koerber mused in a 1943 *Long Trail News*: "...does the green water still tumble down through Clarendon Gorge to fascinate the Long Trailer who pauses on the brink?...Do the chipmunks still reign at Lake Pleiad Camp to hold guard over that smoky stove?...These are a few of the things a soldier thinks about when the going gets tough and the future hazy."

Theron Dean Shelter in the late 1930s, John Vondell and thirsty hiker (unidentified) on the porch.

When the war finally ended, GMC members could once again turn their attention to the Long Trail. Wind and weather had taken their toll, war-time lumbering obscured the trail in places, blazes needed painting, trail signs were down, and the Carmel, Cooley Glen, and Hazen's Notch shelters required extensive repairs. Leaders "earnestly urged" section members to get the trail in shape, so as to "not let the users of the Long Trail down." Slowly, they made the Long Trail passable, and in 1946 the first postwar guidebook appeared.

Three years later, on September 6, 1949, James Taylor, father of the Long Trail, died at age seventy-seven. Having broken his hip the previous winter, he was no longer able to hike. On a beautiful fall day, he rented a boat at Sandbar on Lake Champlain and rowed out as he had on other occasions. Late that afternoon the empty boat drifted ashore. His body was found six days later. Louis Puffer wrote in the *Long Trail News* that no one will ever know what happened, "though it is not hard to guess." Taylor's friends in the Burlington Section passed a resolution praising his "untiring and sacrificial devotion, through so many years and to so many public welfare causes," pledging to carry out his "splendid purposes for our club."

LAURA
COWLES
TRAIL

THE POSTWAR YEARS

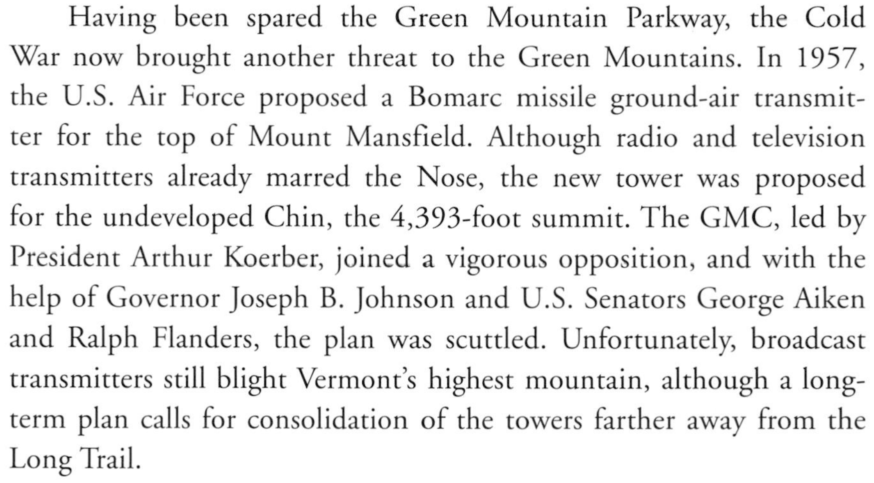

Having been spared the Green Mountain Parkway, the Cold War now brought another threat to the Green Mountains. In 1957, the U.S. Air Force proposed a Bomarc missile ground-air transmitter for the top of Mount Mansfield. Although radio and television transmitters already marred the Nose, the new tower was proposed for the undeveloped Chin, the 4,393-foot summit. The GMC, led by President Arthur Koerber, joined a vigorous opposition, and with the help of Governor Joseph B. Johnson and U.S. Senators George Aiken and Ralph Flanders, the plan was scuttled. Unfortunately, broadcast transmitters still blight Vermont's highest mountain, although a long-term plan calls for consolidation of the towers farther away from the Long Trail.

Skiing became a widely popular sport after World War II, and ski areas like Stratton Mountain (above) proliferated on the slopes of the Green Mountains.

Opposite, top: Looking north from Camel's Hump to Mount Mansfield in winter.

Bottom: A group of winter hikers in the 1950s in typical garb.

Following spread: The Long Trail traverses many magical forest stands. This evergreen grove is on Mount Abraham.

In the postwar decades, tourism grew to become a major Vermont industry, and outdoor recreation, especially alpine skiing, was an essential part of the draw. New ski resorts developed in the 1950s and 1960s — Mount Snow, Okemo, Killington, Jay, Burke, Sugarbush, and Stratton — while older ones, such as Mount Mansfield, Pico, and Mad River Glen, held on or expanded.

GMC leaders, conceding that the Long Trail was neither designed for nor blazed for winter use, stopped trying to attract skiers, although local sections continued to offer ski and snowshoe outings on their winter calendars.

The ski resorts built more than trails and lifts in the Green Mountains. Whole villages of vacation homes sprouted in the foothills, seemingly overnight. Concerned, Governor Deane C. Davis appointed a commission to study the rampant growth. The result was Vermont's 1969 landmark State Land Use and Development Plan, known as Act 250. It established the Vermont Environmental Board and district environmental commissions to assess and control development of more than ten acres, or ten or more home units.

The law restricted land use above 2,500 feet — which included much of the Long Trail. Shirley Strong, a native of Craftsbury and the first woman president of the GMC, was instrumental in getting that provision included. She and her allies wisely campaigned for the mountains, not against development per se: "We need to go positive," she wrote. "We need to start thinking about how important mountains are."

TAYLOR LODGE
1926-1951-1978
Dedicated to
James P. Taylor
under of the G.M.C.
NOTICE
GREEN MOUNTAIN CLUB
VERMONT

THE HIKING BOOM

In 1960, the GMC celebrated its fiftieth anniversary. The Vermont General Assembly, in a joint resolution, thanked it for "a job well done" and expressed its "good wish for the Green Mountain Club's continued success." Membership stood at a healthy 1,500, with 400 in the Killington Section and 300 in the New York Section, the club's two largest chapters. Judge Cowles, whose wife, Laura, was an active hiker and past Burlington Section president, pointed out that membership was about equally divided between men and women. Annual weeklong intersectional meetings attracted large crowds (234 in 1964) who camped, hiked, and broke bread together. Yet, for all its apparent vigor, the GMC was not prepared for the approaching hiking boom.

Now easily accessible by interstate highway, Vermont had become a sanctuary in the Northeast for those wishing to escape the social ferment of the 1960s and 1970s, a haven for the young back-to-nature movement. To Laura and Guy Waterman, who themselves left New York City to homestead in Vermont, "it seemed as if an entire generation wanted to 'find itself' in the backcountry."

And many of them wanted to hike. The physical impact of thousands of heavy lug soles soon became apparent. In one year, an estimated 150,000 people stepped out on the Long Trail, eroding and widening it. (A startling 118 hiked it end-to-end in 1975, the highest number since the GMC began keeping track in 1943.) Overnight shelters filled to capacity, improvised tent sites sprang up, and privies overflowed. Inexperienced hikers tramped on fragile alpine vegetation, lost control of wood fires and backpacking stoves, polluted sources of drinking water, and left dumps of litter behind. The Long Trail was being loved to death.

Nan Dove, the unofficial caretaker of Barrows Camp, reviews the camp register in this 1973 photo.

Opposite: During hiking's boom years, a new sign, rededicating Taylor Lodge to GMC Founder James Taylor, was unveiled by GMC officials. The ceremony took place on September 2, 1978.

Startled, the Green Mountain Club reacted to the onslaught on several fronts to protect the trail and to improve the hiking experience. It discouraged spring hiking until the trails had dried out, first on Camel's Hump, then on all peaks. It urged hikers to carry out what they carried in: "Take nothing but pictures, leave nothing but footprints" was the slogan. It directed the seasonal Long Trail Patrol to build permanent water bars, puncheons, and stone steps in the most vulnerable spots. It revived a 1930s caretaker program, employing young GMC ambassadors/educators at heavily used overnight sites, such as Stratton Pond and Taft Lodge. It worked closely with officials at

the Vermont Department of Forests, Parks, and Recreation, eventually taking over and expanding the Ranger-naturalist Program that parks director Rodney A. Barber had initiated on Mount Mansfield and Camel's Hump. It began an "adopter" program, with volunteers maintaining designated miles of trail or a shelter or lodge. It built new composting privies, which have become models for managing human waste in the backcountry. It published the first *Day Hiker's Guide to Vermont* (1978), edited by George Pearlstein, which encouraged hikers to explore trails beyond the Long Trail system.

The GMC's efforts — helped by a strengthening environmental movement and increasing public awareness of finite natural resources — have shown results. Today's hikers are more aware of their potential impact on the Long Trail and the Vermont landscape. Most know and adhere to the "Leave No Trace" outdoor ethics, which include doing "the rock walk" around alpine plants on the highest summits. Staff members regularly teach these principles, as well as more hands-on backcountry skills, at club headquarters. Since 1995 the GMC has employed an education coordinator, and hiker education has become one of its major programs.

Before paid executive directors and staff, the club's membership, records, and correspondence were maintained by loyal volunteers like Minerva Hinchey of Rutland, who served as corresponding secretary for twenty-two years.

Opposite: Images from the 1960s and 1970s: Group at top right on Mansfield summit includes Jan Abbott (left, standing), club president Shirley Strong (center, behind sign, wearing glasses), and Harris Abbott (standing, right of sign). Top, left: lodge construction in the 1950s. Bottom, left: Much of the promotion of the trail was done by Green Mountain National Forest rangers. Bottom, right: children enjoy a campfire.

THE MATURING OF THE GMC

The impact of the hiking boom meant that the GMC and its Long Trail could no longer be managed only by volunteers, although hundreds of dedicated members continue to serve on the board of directors, on committees, and as trail workers. A full-time executive director and professional staff replaced part-time corresponding secretaries, who had also served as business managers: Lula Tye for twenty-nine years and Minerva Hinchey for twenty-two, until she retired in 1977 at age eighty-two.

Larry Van Meter became the GMC's first executive director in 1977. He was followed by Stephen Rice, Harry Peet, Frederic Preston, Dennis Shaffer, and Ben Rose. Today, the GMC employs ten people year-round, as well as several more seasonal trail workers, mostly college students.

The club had been headquartered in Rutland, a railroad hub and home to early club leaders, since its incorporation in 1917. In 1977, the GMC moved north to a rented office in Montpelier. In the modern world of state and federal regulations, the club found it needed to be closer to the seat of government. Then in 1992, having outgrown the Montpelier space and wishing to be nearer the Long Trail, the club purchased the former 1836 May Farm property on Route 100 in Waterbury Center, where its headquarters is located today. The south barn burned in 2003 and was replaced in 2009 after a successful capital campaign. The GMC campus includes offices, a hiker center, meeting and retail space, tool workshop and storage, and seasonal housing for trail and shelter workers.

THE PROTECTOR OF THE LONG TRAIL

If maintaining the Long Trail had become a bigger challenge than in the past, so had protecting it. Initially, a handshake between James P. Taylor and a landowner was sufficient to allow Long Trail hikers to traverse private property. In the 1980s, club leaders woke up to a different world.

While the southern part of the trail lay safely on state and federal lands, in the north it mostly crossed private tracts, much of it owned by big lumber companies. A slump in the timber market and increasing property taxes led to economic pressure to sell forest properties. High-elevation land—which meant the Long Trail—was first to be put on the market. Suddenly, large parcels that included 32 miles of the Long Trail in Lamoille, Franklin, and Orleans Counties were for sale, with another 30 miles at risk. There was no guarantee that future landowners, as in former days, would honor hikers' rights-of-way.

In July 1971, young Deborah Abbott became a human signpost at the junction of the Cliff Trail and the Long Trail on Mount Mansfield. The club was collecting information on how hikers got to the summit ridge, and Deborah got their attention!

Alarmed, in 1986 the GMC board of directors, under the leadership of President Preston J. Bristow and Executive Director Harry T. Peet, launched the Long Trail Protection Campaign. Its ambitious goal was the permanent protection of the trail through land acquisition and perpetual easement. It was a major turning point in the history of the GMC.

The GMC found broad support for the capital campaign, which raised the club's profile. Membership soon passed five thousand—testimony to the Long Trail's importance to Vermonters and hikers everywhere.

Having only limited experience in fund-raising, however, club leaders quickly realized that they needed professional help. They found the right person in Robert L. Lincoln, who was hired in 1987 to direct the fund-raising. Lincoln retired in 2008.

Hundreds of individuals and businesses contributed to the Long Trail Protection Fund. Those able to part with $1,000 or more were enrolled in the 265-Mile Club—265 miles then being the length of the Long Trail. One significant member of the 265-Mile Club is the Derby Elementary School whose students raised money for the trail with their "Sponsor a Tree" project. Other fund-raising efforts were an auction, a statewide Hike-a-Thon, and pledges collected by Robert Northrop for two end-to-end Long Trail hikes celebrating his seventy-fifth and eightieth birthdays.

Trail register and fall foliage on Harmon Hill near Bennington.

FURTHER READING

Jane and Will Curtis and Frank Lieberman, *Green Mountain Adventure: Vermont's Long Trail* (Montpelier: Green Mountain Club, 1985).

Laura and Guy Waterman, *Forest and Crag: A History of Hiking, Trail Blazing, and Adventure in the Northeast Mountains* (Boston: Appalachian Mountain Club Books, 1989, 2003).

Beginning in 1986, the Vermont Legislature, under the leadership of Senators Robert Gannett and Richard Mazza, allocated funds annually for Long Trail land purchases. The first acquisition with the Long Trail Protection Fund was the 171-acre Riendeau Tract on the Canadian border, secured for $20,000. The Nature Conservancy assisted with this and many subsequent Long Trail land transactions.

Club leaders initially estimated that somewhat less than $2 million raised over five years would be sufficient to protect the Long Trail. The task proved to be much more daunting. In its first twenty years, the campaign protected 60 miles of the Long Trail and 18 miles of side trails, while preserving 24,000 acres of land from development, at a cost of $9 million. The GMC transferred most of the land to the state of Vermont.

Given the time and expertise required to negotiate land acquisitions, right-of-way easements, and conservation restrictions, the Green Mountain Club decided it needed a land protection coordinator. With a grant from the state, it was able to hire Susan Shea in 1990. Shea stayed in the position for fifteen years, building relationships with all Long Trail landowners, whether their land was on the market or not.

Today, after more than twenty years of work, the Long Trail Protection Campaign is nearing its goal of permanently protecting the Long Trail for future generations.

◆

In its first hundred years, the GMC has evolved from a small, idealistic group of pioneer trail builders into a large, well-respected organization of almost ten thousand members. It has successfully adapted itself from being "just" a trail club to a modern, many-faceted organization that is also a government partner, educator, environmental advocate, and land steward. And throughout its long history, it has managed to stay true to James P. Taylor's vision of "making the Vermont mountains play a larger part in the life of the people."

Opposite: Looking east from the Long Trail north of Montclair Glen.

CHAPTER 3

LIFE ON THE TRAIL, THEN AND NOW

The Evolution of Hiking Styles, Equipment, and Ethics

BY TOM SLAYTON

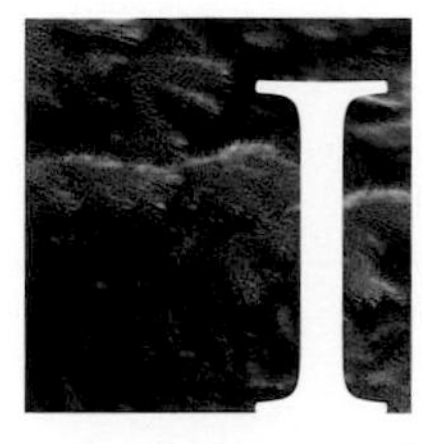

IN THE PHOTOGRAPHS made by Theron S. Dean, we see a near-mythical moment in time—the earliest days of the Green Mountain Club (GMC).

Because of the cumbersome photographic equipment available when he took his photographs in the first few decades of the twentieth century, there are not many shots of actual hiking. Instead, Dean captured many commemorative moments: cookouts or groups of hikers preparing to head down the Long Trail or clustered on a mountaintop. There are views of the trail that the GMC was then in the process of building, even a few photographs of the construction itself. And Dean carefully documented special places along the trail—caves and cliffs, campsites and cabins, plus scenic views of Camel's Hump and Mount Mansfield from afar.

Although the mountains still demand effort, today's hikers have the advantage of frame packs, waterproof fabrics, and lightweight boots.

Theron Dean was not the only photographer of life along the Long Trail in its earliest days, but he was the most prolific and probably the most determined. There are now hundreds of his images preserved as glass slides in the Special Collections Department of the University of Vermont's Bailey-Howe Library. Taken together, these images constitute an incomparable historical resource. They are the major visual documentation of the earliest years of the GMC and the Long Trail.

At first glance, they seem to depict a strange and motley crew: women hikers in long skirts and "flapper" hats, men in puttees and high-laced boots, many of them wearing neckties and wool sport jackets. Later, the garb becomes less strange, but it still speaks of a different era: knickers and middy blouses instead of shorts and T-shirts; Adirondack pack baskets and tumplines instead of aluminum frame packs with waistbands. There are several photographs of men carefully lathering and shaving at shelters along the trail. Beards are common only on elderly men.

Yet the more one studies these photographs — and reads the hiking journals of the day — the more one feels a kinship with these early pioneers of Vermont hiking and trail making. The mountains are, after all, a great equalizer. Despite the undeniable difference in styles, the experience of the people Theron Dean photographed was really not that much different from our experience in the Green Mountains today.

What was different was the hiking and camping ethic. But more on that later.

The GMC had been formed in 1910 "to make the Vermont mountains play a larger part in the life of the people." By the time Dean began snapping his photographs, about four or five years after that, it was quite evident that the club was succeeding in its mission. Wherever Dean pointed his camera, in whatever season of the year — winter included — he caught Vermonters and their friends out enjoying the life of the mountains.

Camera-inspired horseplay atop Camel's Hump in 1928.

Opposite: Equipment in the 1920s was definitely nonstandard. The group preparing to climb Camel's Hump (top) hiked in everything from high-top boots and puttees to street flats and cloche hats. Will Monroe is seated, third from left. An only slightly less eclectic collection of clothing and equipment is seen in the seven overnight campers at the first Glen Ellen Shelter in the lower photo.

Dean may have begun his photography for his own pleasure, but he very quickly found a useful purpose for his hobby. Well before the club's tenth birthday, he had assembled a show of glass lantern slides made from his photographs and was using it to introduce the Long Trail and the GMC to the nonhiking public. One advertisement for the lecture declared that on May 16, 1918, Dean would speak and show slides at the Massachusetts Institute of Technology in Boston. The subject was "A Week's Tramp in the Green Mountains."

The advertisement promised that Dean would show more than one hundred lantern slides, "many of which are colored,"— that is, hand-painted with transparent color — depicting the beautiful scenery of the Green Mountains, trail building, snowshoeing, and trail shelters. "His lecture will cover 50 miles of the most scenic part of the Long Trail, from Lincoln Mountain to Smugglers' Notch on Mount Mansfield, passing over four peaks more than 4,000 feet high," it declared.

Glen Ellen Lodge

Theron Dean, his hefty pack filled with wool clothing and camera equipment, is shown on a winter trek in a hand-colored glass slide made from one of his many photographs.

Dean's slide show and lecture would, in other words, entertain his audience with photographs of the exciting world just then being opened in the heart of Vermont's Green Mountains. As it turned out, he not only gave the Long Trail and the GMC some much-needed publicity, he also created an invaluable visual record of the early years of the GMC—and helped promote the first great rush of enthusiasm for mountain recreation in Vermont.

Who were the people who turned up in Theron Dean's photographs? They were certainly an eclectic-looking bunch, and it was obvious that many of them were new to mountain sports. In a 1920 shot of a group preparing to climb Camel's Hump, some of the men in the party are wearing spectacularly high-laced leather boots and leggings that rise to the knee. Others have sturdy work shoes. But several in the party are equipped only with low street shoes, which would give virtually no support on the Hump's rocky trails. Most of the men, in that more formal era, are sporting short neckties, and one woman appears ready to attempt the hike in a skirt, street pumps, and a cloche hat. Will Monroe, leader of the hike, sits off to one side, head bowed, perhaps wondering how he is going to get this band of dudes up and down the mountain in one piece.

Several of Dean's photos document the heroic amounts of work it took to clean and establish the trail. One hand-colored slide shows two young men and a boy in knickers heaving rocks into place to build a trail bed across the steep south face of Camel's Hump. Unlike the party of beginners, these volunteers are clad in gear recognizable to hikers today: sweaters, work clothes, and sturdy, ankle-high boots. In other photos, hikers wearing belt axes and carrying bucksaws stand atop shattered piles of timber, prepared to saw and hack their way through the tangled mass of blowdowns down to solid earth.

Winter hikers at Bolton Lodge prior to World War II.

WINTER WAS NO BARRIER

Winter apparently didn't slow the GMC's first-generation members down at all. Dean's photographs clearly document the considerable amount of winter hiking that they were engaged in during the club's first fifteen or so years. Many photos show hikers strapping on wooden snowshoes, stomping their way up snowy ravines, and exulting at a handy hiking lodge or on a snowy summit. Dean himself appears in several of these photos. (In one, apparently snapped by his friend, Louis Puffer, he struggles to emerge from a snowy hole in the rocks just below Stark's Wall that Monroe, with his penchant for naming virtually every identifiable feature of the mountain landscape, had christened "Dean's Cave." It was obvious that Dean and many other early club members relished winter outings.)

Their enthusiasm was doubly notable because most of them lacked any specialized winter clothing. In those far-off days before the advent of lightweight synthetic-fabric outer garments, wool—and plenty of it—kept them warm. An early photo of GMC founder James P. Taylor (page 14) shows him clutching snowshoes with heavy mittens and wearing at least three layers of woolen clothing (probably over wool long johns), topped off with a knit woolen cap. Despite the snowy day, he's plenty warm. His outer garment, a heavy Johnson Woolen Mill–type jacket, is unbuttoned, and his necktie has been loosened.

Judge Clarence Cowles, another GMC pioneer, was as intrepid as any contemporary winter sportsman. He apparently loved being out in the mountains in winter. It is Cowles, along with Leroy Little and Herbert Wheaton Congdon, who is credited with the first winter ascent of Mount Mansfield, on February 21, 1920.

Cowles liked to camp out in the snowy Green Mountains. For clothing on his winter forays, he wore, he wrote, "a wool union suit, sweater, business coat with the collar turned up, cap with ear flaps, wool socks and mittens." To keep warm, even on the coldest days, he said, "I simply kept going vigorously."

Marion Urie, equipped for her 1933 end-to-end hike with Lucile Pelsue. Note pistol holster on her belt.

Rugged as Cowles and the other GMC winter hikers may have been, they were more than matched by their female compatriots, several of whom climbed the mountains in winter wearing long woolen skirts! And it is notable that several of the Long Trail's first end-to-enders were women. There were the famous "Three Musketeers" who completed the trail in 1927. And in 1933, the plucky duo of Marion Urie and Lucile Pelsue followed suit.

HIKING WITH MARION AND LUCILE

Marion Urie, pretty, stylish, and slender as a willow wand, was also a good writer. Her notebooks and the charming account of her trip that she later published in *The Vermonter* give a vivid picture of life on the Long Trail in the 1920s and 1930s.

Even though they made their trip in the early summer, the two women were thorough believers in the Gospel of Wool. They wore part-wool underwear, wool whipcord riding trousers, wool flannel Army shirts, and heavy wool socks. "Many of our friends were amazed at this display of woolen clothing for a hike in the middle of summer," Urie wrote, "but it is the most desirable type of clothing to wear as the soft woolens absorb the perspiration and are a protection against the cool winds of the mountain tops."

Opposite: These photos from the scrapbook of Louis B. Puffer document adventures from the GMC's first ten years. In the top photo, J. Laurence Griswold (left) and Puffer are shown by a roadside in 1910. Below, unidentified hikers tend a campfire at the DuFresne Job in 1919.

She confided also that on their belts, each of the women carried, in addition to a knife, a light ax, and a canteen, one piece of decidedly nonregulation equipment: a .32 Colt automatic pistol! "The pistol was carried chiefly as a means of killing porcupines," she explained, adding blithely, "or any other pest that sought our company too persistently." How did other hikers respond to meeting two armed women in the woods? Miss Urie reported only that comments on the pistols from people she met were "varied and amusing."

In many ways the young women's experience was not unlike that of contemporary long-distance hikers on the Long Trail. They

Long Trailers of the Early Days; J.L.G. and L.B.P. on a Hike from Mass. to Canada in July 1910.

When the Trail was Young,- Boiling the Kettle at the DuFresne Job, back in 1919.

Rufus Thompson, Clark Thayer, Ralph Van Meter, and R. L. Coffin are shown as they crossed Route 30 in southern Vermont on a hike in August 1936.

ate oatmeal, macaroni and cheese, prunes, rice, and chocolate (among other foods); they got wet when it rained and on dry days sometimes had to search long and hard for water; they battled porcupines and mice from time to time and had their spirits lifted by the beauty of the mountain forests and the long views they enjoyed.

But there were differences as well. The two women had none of the lightweight outerwear common today. They wore rubberized Army ponchos and white linen hats to ward off the inevitable rain; they carried belt axes in order to rustle up firewood for the evening campfire (a luxury now strongly discouraged), and they experienced the beauty of the Green Mountains when the mountains were almost completely wild—no ski areas, very few paved roads traversing them, no high-altitude resort homes.

"There is the constant thrill of never knowing just what is coming next," Urie wrote, "Every curve reveals some new charm or unique

These hikers are staying warm as best they can on a winter outing to Taft Lodge in 1929. Louis B. Puffer, who took the photograph, notes that the weather was "coolish."

specimen. Perhaps it is a huge rock capped with lovely little ferns growing in a deep bed of moss; or it may be a weather-beaten tree, twisted and gnarled into a most fantastic shape. At other times the trail comes out on some natural promontory or lookout, and the hiker sees spread before him a vast panorama of forest with the farms and villages nestled in the valley below."

Urie recalled the old saying "the longest way 'round is the sweetest way home," and applied it to the Long Trail: ". . . this footpath winds and curves continually. In most cases, this is all for the good, as it makes it possible to include many more beautiful spots than could be seen otherwise."

Urie and Pelsue did the trail the hard way—starting on the Canadian border and hiking southward. Even so, they made the journey in five fewer days than their predecessors, the Three Musketeers, who took thirty-three days to travel from Massachusetts to Canada.

AFTER WORLD WAR II

With the coming of World War II, the era of high boots and puttees, wool-on-wool clothing, and white linen hats came to an end. It took a couple years after the war to get the Long Trail back—to clear away four years worth of underbrush and blowdowns, repaint the directional signs, spruce up the shelters, and so on. But in the late 1940s and 1950s, a new generation discovered the Green Mountains and returned to the Long Trail.

The Long Trail near Hazen's Notch looks much as it has for the past half century and more.

By then, many of the first-generation hikers of the GMC had passed on or become too infirm to hike. A new wave of hikers in their twenties, thirties, and forties was finding its way into the woods. Blue jeans and plaid flannel shirts replaced knickers and knee socks. Adirondack pack baskets gave way to pack frames and (later) internal-frame packs. Tan Dunham work boots were the footwear of choice.

"For footwear, we wore whatever we'd normally wear to go hunting or out in the barn," said Smith Edwards of Jericho who began hiking in the postwar years. "Nobody that I knew wore boots specially designed for hiking," He recalled that hiking clothes were just everyday outdoor wear. "Used to be, you made that wool shirt do as a rain shirt or whatever. Today, you've got three different shirts—and nobody knew anything about fast-drying nylon hiking shorts!"

Bill Walker of Westfield, New Jersey, prepares to move out on the Long Trail in the late 1930s.

Edwards and other longtime GMC members said a lot of their equipment was improvised from what they might have lying around their home or farm. A blanket sewed up or held together with safety pins would do for a sleeping bag. Boy Scout knapsacks and cooking kits (folding aluminum fry pan, small lidded pot, and cup) and Army canteens that hung on the belt were all common.

Doris Washburn of East Montpelier sewed up an old comforter as her sleeping bag and carried her gear in a small canvas Boy Scout knapsack. She and others said that their food was simple and mostly made from supermarket components—packaged soups, macaroni and cheese, and the like. Edwards agreed: "There's just too much old Yankee in me to use freeze-dried when I can make just about anything I want out of supermarket stuff."

Nevertheless, all the old-timers remember those days warmly. Like their trail food, GMC social events were simple, informal, and outdoorsy—with emphasis on the outdoorsy. Just about everyone recalled winter oyster stew hikes and summer intersectional campouts.

Harris and Jan Abbott said that the winter oyster stew hikes were a regular activity of the Burlington Section in the 1950s and 1960s. The Montpelier Section also organized some oyster stews, and there are some who remembered those events even farther back in time.

The Burlington Section oyster stews were typical, according to the Abbotts. All that was required for a tasty oyster stew was oysters, milk, and butter. People would pack in tightly capped jars of oysters and jugs of milk, most often to Taylor Lodge on the south flank of Mount Mansfield in Nebraska Notch. But other items added complications.

"Packing in the pies was... interesting," Jan Abbott said. (Pies had to be tied on and kept horizontal so the filling wouldn't spill inside one's pack.) Eventually, though, the oyster events became too popular — the Abbotts remembered one such event that attracted upwards of seventy hikers! "It took a tremendous amount of wood to warm the stew," she recalled. Also, the price of oysters went up sharply. So after several years, they were quietly discontinued.

INTERSECTIONAL GATHERINGS

Recipe for happiness: a friend, a dog, and a great day in the mountains. Photo taken in early 1960s.

Intersectional campouts each summer provided an inexpensive camping vacation for some and a way to complete their end-to-end hike of the Long Trail for others. They were usually held at a Boy Scout or Girl Scout camp near the mountains. Each year, a different section of the trail would be focused on, car drops would be arranged, and people would hike the portions of the trail they needed to complete. Doris Washburn was able to do the entire trail in four years by going to intersectionals, she said. She completed the last section of her end-to-end in 1967.

In addition to the hikes, intersectionals offered evening talks or slide shows, as well as other activities. One notice promised "swimming, hiking, loafing, badminton and volleyball for the tirelessly energetic." Once when the event was held in Plymouth, participants panned for gold, though there is no record of any fortunes being made. It was like a week or ten-day summer camp for adults as well as children.

"It wasn't expensive," Washburn said. "A family could come with three or four children and have a great time for fifty dollars." It cost fifty cents per person per night to camp, and meals were inexpensive and cooked over a camp stove or open fire. "Stone Soup" events, where everyone would contribute a can of something or other and share in the (always unique) result, were popular and made the week affordable for many. "People just didn't have a lot of money then, so you either had to go sponge off your relatives or go camping," Jan Abbott said.

Even so, everyone recalled the intersectionals as wonderful events. There was no drinking or rowdy partying, just good, homemade fun. "The camaraderie was just incredible," Abbott recalled. "And you could get your end-to-end because there were people who would spot cars for you."

A spring hike in the 1950s on Mount Mansfield. Note clothing and equipment of the era.

Intersectionals began around 1960 and continued strong for about twenty years. But then the school year was lengthened to begin in August, vacation patterns changed, and those gatherings came to an end.

It was in that same era that hiking and camping suddenly surged in popularity, and the Long Trail began to feel the caress of too many lug-soled boots. With the sharply increased use of the Long Trail and shelters came rising concern about what the impact of exponentially increasing numbers of hikers was doing to the forest — especially the trail itself and areas around the shelters. Change was again coming to the Green Mountains, and this time the agents of change were the hikers themselves.

Looking south from Mount Mansfield summit, towards Camel's Hump.

A CHANGE IN HIKING ETHICS

The hiking boom of the 1960s and 1970s nearly overwhelmed the Long Trail. The number of people hiking surged dramatically, with as many as 150,000 people using the trail in a single year. The damage suddenly being done by the increased numbers was startling — fragile mountaintop alpine areas were pounded into mud, shelter sites were stripped of any semblance of firewood for hundreds of yards in every direction, trash dumps and outhouses overflowed. As noted elsewhere in this book, the GMC responded to this new crisis in a number of ways — educational programs, caretakers on mountaintops and at key huts, composting privies, and so on. But for the hikers themselves, the increased popularity of their favorite sport meant a new hiking ethic. They would have to change their ways; the era of low-impact backpacking had, of necessity, arrived.

Outhouse messages epitomize Long Trail humor.

Opposite, top: With campfires a thing of the past, cooking is now done on light, packable gas-fired stoves.

Bottom: A party of 1960s hikers watches their step in an alpine summit area.

Perhaps the most obvious change (and the one most lamented by the earlier hikers) was that campfires, the universal symbol of the outdoor life, had to go. Likewise, woodstoves that had warmed many a winter snowshoe party were removed from most huts. There just weren't enough trees in the forest to provide heat, light, and cooking fuel for the vastly increased army of hikers. (And according to GMC executive director Ben Rose, there was another problem with the woodstoves also: The camps that had stoves had a tendency to burn down.)

Spruce-bough beds, which had been the standard of backwoods comfort prior to World War II, were now forbidden, and the admonition, familiar to every shelter user along the Long Trail, to "leave some wood for the next party," was abandoned. Backpackers were urged to carry lightweight gas stoves for cooking and foam sleeping pads to cushion their bunks, and gradually those changes were accepted.

The trash dumps that were a feature of most trailside camps and shelters were dug up and removed. The closing of the dumps coincided with a campaign to reeducate hikers to dispose of their own trash — off trail. "Carry in, carry out" became the new trail mantra, and as a result, canned food virtually disappeared as a Long Trail camping staple.

Not everyone thought the changes were a great idea. The new regulations chafed at some of the more independent old-timers, and others grumbled about the loss of the simple pleasures of an evening campfire or a wood-heated cabin in midwinter. Was it really necessary?

LONG TRAIL NEWS

LONG TRAIL NEWS

NOVEMBER, 1941

The *Long Trail News*, official newsletter of the GMC, has evolved typographically since its earliest days. Here are some of the various versions.

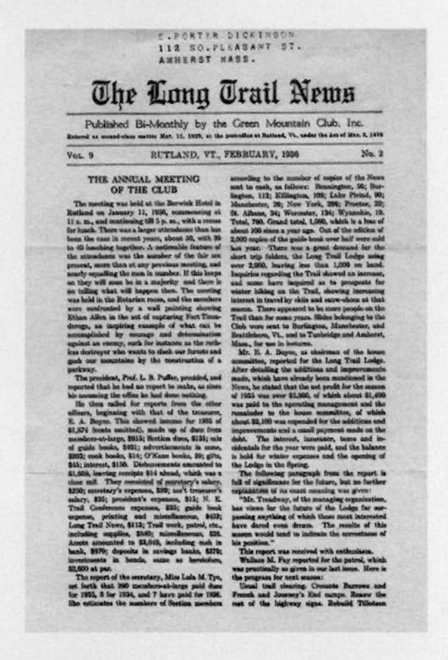
The Long Trail News

Published Bi-Monthly by the Green Mountain Club, Inc.

Vol. 9 RUTLAND, VT., FEBRUARY, 1936 No. 2

THE ANNUAL MEETING OF THE CLUB

The Long Trail News

Volunteerism is Alive and Well At GMC

Long Trail NEWS

Roderick Rice of Burlington still feels that today's hikers miss a lot of the fun of those earlier outings. He recalled winter outings with other members of the Burlington Section. "We'd take off after church on Sunday and climb up to Butler Lodge [on Mount Mansfield's west side], and toast cheese sandwiches over the stove," he said. "Then we'd hike back down in the dark."

The woodstoves that were then a feature of every closed camp or lodge made winter hikes not only fun but, in some cases, possible. "Dave Otis and I used to get out and go in the winter," Rice said. "We'd snowshoe in a couple of miles. We never had any special equipment, but we figured we could get warmed up by building a fire in one of the camp stoves."

It's really too bad, he said, that those kinds of outings had to come to an end. Rice may have had a special reason for recalling those days with affection: he met his wife, Emily, when he was caretaker of Bolton Lodge, right after World War II. Emily had been invited by a friend to "go for a hike," and by chance, the two young women chose to climb up to Bolton Lodge. Emily was originally from Little Rock, Arkansas, and was working in Burlington at the time. "I didn't know anything about hiking," she noted. "I said, 'What's a hike?'"

A romance flourished between the hiking novice and the young caretaker at Bolton Lodge, and in 1947, Rod and Emily were married. "We had our honeymoon at Bryant's lower camp [a hikers cabin not

Hiker on Deer Leap Mountain looks across Sherburne Pass to the ski trails on Pico Peak.

Opposite: Hikers crossing Route 103 near Clarendon.

far from Bolton Lodge], and on New Year's Eve, the Green Mountain Club came up and we had a little party."

However, by the 1980s, times had changed, and the older, more romantic style of hiking was becoming a thing of the past. The GMC's educational programs were successful, and the new hiking ethic was accepted. The crackling and flickering light of the campfire (and the smoke, it must be admitted) were replaced by the hissing of small backpacking stoves. Hikers carried trash bags. Gradually, over a period of years, the forest returned and erased the bombed-out look of most backwoods shelters, and the tiny, fragile alpine plants reestablished themselves on the mountaintops of Vermont.

CHANGE...AND CONTINUITY

Other changes had come to Vermont's mountains as well. Hiker numbers subsided from the frantic heyday of the 1970s and 1980s, but were still substantially above prewar years. Ski areas had proliferated and expanded, and so ski trails intersected the Long Trail in several places. The rumble of ski lifts was heard in the winter, and at least one beloved Vermont mountain—Jay Peak—acquired a large tramway terminal right on its rocky summit. Mountain streams that once were pure had become suspect—giardia and other parasites were widespread—and hikers could no longer assume that drinking from a mountain stream was safe.

At the same time, hiking equipment became much more lightweight and sophisticated. Boots designed specifically for hiking on rocky trails gave better support and greater purchase than the old work shoes. Nylon rain gear was not only lighter than the old U.S. Army ponchos—it actually kept most of the rain out! Water purification systems and plastic water bottles replaced the belt-worn Army canteens. And there are now almost as many different kinds of camp stoves and cooking outfits as there are campers to use them.

But in deeper ways, the experience of hiking the Long Trail may not have changed that drastically. Most of the trail is still primitive and unspoiled. Hiking it is still a rugged, often transformative experience.

The murmuring forest surrounds the hiker for miles—for hours or days, depending on the length of his or her journey. Thanks to the genius of its builders, the trail still presents an ever-changing array of beauty, winding through woodsy glens alive with wildflowers and birdsong, clambering up rocky ledges through dark boreal forests to emerge suddenly on a bare mountaintop with a view that seems to go on forever. Then back into the woods again, for miles and more miles.

And it has to be said that the Green Mountains can be tough. The rain falls on just and unjust hikers alike. And even in dry years, it seems to fall regularly enough to keep a long-distance hiker's feet wet most of the time. Some of the Long Trail's uphill grades are legendary— steep, rocky, and unrelenting. And not all shelters are cozy retreats. They can be wet and overcrowded, despite the best efforts of the GMC trail patrol to keep up with the forces of time, weather, and entropy.

Yet even so, people still write of their experiences on the trail as vital, important, life changing, and beautiful.

Popular camps on the Long Trail are periodically rebuilt.

Opposite: Camel's Hump from the west—serene, unchanging, ever new.

In his book, *Forest Under My Fingernails*, Walt McLaughlin documents an end-to-end trip in 1998 that left him thin and exhausted, but deeply satisfied and reluctant to leave, even after he had reached the Canadian border.

"The forest is under my fingernails," McLaughlin wrote, "A mountain stream runs through me. I am no less wild than a bear or a moose. Things that were important to me a month ago no longer matter. I am free — as free as any creature can be within the brackets of immortality."

In those words, we hear the voices of James P. Taylor and Clarence Cowles, Theron Dean and Marion Urie. And the ever-present, siren song of Vermont's high-altitude mountain pathway — the Long Trail.

Above: Hiker near Sterling Pond.
Right: Summit mist and clouds on Mount Mansfield.

WOMEN OF THE LONG TRAIL

I would like to start all over again... and maybe I shall. All together the Long Trail is as near to heaven as most of us get in this life.

—Violet May Hall, 1948

BY LAURA WATERMAN

My husband, Guy, and I had the great pleasure of meeting two of the Three Musketeers by chance on October 10, 1981. We were immersed in research for our Northeast mountain history, *Forest and Crag*, and on that day drove to Derby Center to interview Helen Wiley at an inn where she was staying.

She had promised to tell us her mountain memories, which stretched back to the Long Trail in 1921. As our conversation wound down, Helen said she'd like to introduce us to her traveling companions who were hikers too, and in walked Hilda Martin (née Kurth) and Catherine Robbins, both near eighty years of age, but in terms of vitality appearing not a day older than when they had become the first women, along with their friend, Kathleen Norris, to traverse the Long Trail from Williamstown, Massachusetts, to North Troy, Vermont, in 1927. As a result, they became the toast of Vermont—and the nation.

Leigh Hunt cooking at Emily Proctor Shelter.

We made a date to interview Hilda in early November. She lived in Schenectady, New York, in the city row house where she'd grown up. Inside, the high-ceilinged rooms were furnished with family pieces all brought to a high shine. Hilda had placed on the table the scrapbook of her Long Trail hike for us to look at. "They Carried No Firearms, and Had No Male Escort," headlined the *San Francisco Examiner*. The *New York Times* for September 4, 1927, displayed a photograph of the Three Musketeers, as the women were dubbed, wearing knee-high lace-up boots, knickers, bandannas, big grins, and loaded knapsacks on their backs.

Listening to Hilda tell the tale as we thumbed through her scrapbook, the years melted away. We heard how they had mailed food packages ahead to farms along the route so they could keep pack weight

The first women to hike the Long Trail from Massachusetts to Canada were Hilda Kurth, Catherine Robbins, and Kathleen Norris or, as they were nicknamed, the "Three Musketeers." The Musketeers won national publicity for themselves and the Long Trail.

to twenty to twenty-five pounds each, just as through-hikers do today. They slept in blankets at the shelters, and they were "always wet," Hilda told us, especially their boots. But their spirits never dampened.

While women on the Long Trail today could have much the same experience — both in terms of feeling safe and enduring wet feet — the Three Musketeers' thirty-two-day trip was a real pioneering adventure. Near Stratton Mountain, the only way to cross a rushing stream was by crawling across a sixty-foot-high trestle, rotting timbers crumbling beneath their hands. Near Peru Peak, they spent two hours battling a recent blowdown. At Little Rock Pond — today teeming with summertime hikers — they went swimming in solitude, having traveled for six days without meeting a single person. When they hit the northern part of the trail, it was as yet uncut, merely blazed.

In the early days, women end-to-enders were noteworthy — Agnes Watkins published in *The Long Trail News* a full-length story of her 1929 trip with three companions, all out-of-staters. But by 1933 when Marion Urie and Lucile Pelsue became the third female party to complete the trip, their feat was confined to the "Notes" section. (Though Marion later wrote an evocative account of their trip for *The Vermonter* magazine.)

That is as it should be. Hiking the trail for women, if not becoming commonplace by the early 1930s, was no longer a novelty—even for children. Mary Beardsley Fenn had begun hiking the Long Trail with her family in 1927, when she was seven years old. When the Beardsley family finished in 1932, Mary became the youngest end-to-ender on record.

By the 1940s, the end-to-end reports contained testimonials from women who were experimenting with hiking alone. Muriel Grauman wrote of walking from Smugglers' Notch to Taylor Lodge in 1942: "Perhaps the most interesting was the experience of going by myself and being entirely 'on my own' on mountains never previously visited." Violet May Hall, who completed the trail in 1948, wrote: "The part I enjoyed the most...was the week or ten days I spent alone, from French Camp to Jay. It was up there that the old warden on Belvidere told me I was the first hiker, man or woman, thru that summer." Peggy Jones, who completed the trail in 1953, confessed: "I'll have to admit that I've done a lot of the trail alone. I don't recommend it, but there are times when no one else can go when you can, and you go alone. There's something wonderful about walking alone in the woods or making a balky stove cook, or seeing a sunset—the only human in evidence. One has to calculate the risks."

Women join in the hard work of trail building and maintenance on the Long Trail Patrol.

But not every woman liked such solitude, and Doris Washburn, who finished the Long Trail in 1967, reported: "The only section I hiked alone was from the Massachusetts line to Route 9...I think I set a time record there, and I decided I do not like to hike alone!"

For Nancy Kazarian, hiking the Long Trail was a life-changing experience. After finishing in 1982, she wrote: "I've hiked some of the highest mountains in the world but none can compare to the beauty and challenge of the Long Trail. Backpacking had given me the self-confidence I never had, and the ability to push myself a bit further than I thought possible."

This seemed to be the case for four young women who hiked the trail in 1977. On their first day, they wrote: "From Shooting Star became more and more desperate with heat, lack of water, lack of condition, and weight of pack...Frequent collapses, covered with flies...How quickly standards of civilization left us...Could we last the night?" The next day they made only three miles and "spent evening sorting out equipment—eliminating. Even Kathy's deodorant—supreme sacrifice! Eliminated whiskey sours. But Carol A. refused to make her supreme sacrifice—scotch."

Building a youngster's love of the mountains on the Long Trail.

They kept going, falling farther behind their schedule. But despite their struggle, their support of each other was as strong as ever. "All decided we couldn't make it past Montclair... Sat and brewed coffee and more coffee and more coffee. Talked about food. Carol H. learned how to use the stove." On Day 29 they reached the Massachusetts line. "There we adjourned, smelly as we were, to Howard Johnson's. Had fresh salad and a magnificent meal. People gave us funny looks. Sue said some of them even sniffed, but we didn't care—WE HAD MADE IT! We were eating proper food. END TO ENDERS. HURRAH. TOLD YOU WE COULD DO IT!"

From the beginning, the "footpath in the wilderness" was the kind of trail where women felt comfortable and welcomed, yet challenged. Thelma Bonney and Erna Clayton began a series of trips on the Long Trail in which they'd be off for a week or two in the woods, taking in stride whatever the mountain weather threw at them. Thelma's journal for 1933 records an all-day rain:

"...All the way down Killington, it poured. Rain was in our eyes, in our faces, in our hair, in our necks. In our shoes...Erna would be walking ahead, and when I looked at her back—the bulging pack and flopping poncho—I'd have to laugh. We had not a care in the whole wide world. It was raining. We were soaked in spots, but still dry in the vital spots, and we knew we'd have a dry bed and warm food for the night. It was raining and we were in the woods. It was glorious, so we laughed. We looked ridiculous, so we laughed. We were happy, so we laughed."

CHAPTER 4

A TRAIL FOR ANY PACE

The Passion and Pleasure of Hiking in Vermont

BY KATY KLUTZNIK

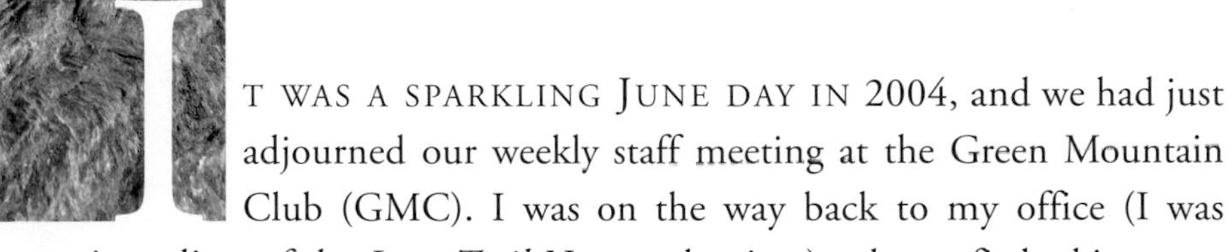

IT WAS A SPARKLING JUNE DAY IN 2004, and we had just adjourned our weekly staff meeting at the Green Mountain Club (GMC). I was on the way back to my office (I was managing editor of the *Long Trail News* at the time), when a fit-looking man with excellent posture bounded into the office and announced that he was planning on breaking the speed record for hiking the Long Trail end-to-end. I looked behind me, wondering if he was talking to someone else. I said, "Um, can I help you with something?" He was aggressive, pointed, obviously determined. He identified himself as "Cave Dog" and seemed to expect I'd know who he was. He wanted to know what the current record was; he wanted to know if his "team" could camp at headquarters; he wanted "support"; he wanted a write-up in the *Long Trail News*.

Opposite: Through-hikers toil up a steep section of trail heading north, toward Clarendon Lookout.

I was dumbfounded. Is there a record? Does anyone care how fast anyone else hikes? Can you actually compare any two Long Trail hikes? I mean, which trail—the one before or after the relocation to Bamforth Ridge on Camel's Hump? And what about direction of travel? Are there northbound and southbound records? And, again, does anyone care? Obviously, Cave Dog did. A few other staff members wandered by, mostly not paying attention. I told him I was sorry, we didn't know anything about records on the trail and couldn't be of much help. I think he said something about the GMC being snooty to a member of the press. He did his end-to-end hike in something like four days that week, and then he was gone. He probably still holds the record.

Sometimes defining a thing by what it's not helps one puzzle out what it is. When Cave Dog turned tail and left the office, I thought, well, that guy definitely isn't a Vermonter (neither am I, technically, but I'm working on it). And he's definitely not a member of the Green Mountain Club. He'll probably never set foot on the trail again after completing his hike (run?). He's off to other records in other states far, far away from the Green Mountains. And we're still here, doing our work to protect and tend our footpath.

But, wait, who are "we"? I'd never fit distinctly into any category or group. At least I didn't think so. But suddenly, in the wake of Cave Dog, I felt a sense of belonging: to Vermont, the GMC, the Long Trail. When I told other staff members about him, no one judged his endeavor; most seemed nonplussed and quickly resumed work on something that seemed more important.

At first, as I contemplated my own attachment to the Long Trail, I imagined myself on the pole opposite Cave Dog. For me, hiking on the Long Trail was about slowness, contemplation, spiritual communion with nature. Later that same summer, though, I became interested in hiking farther on my day hikes. And faster. At times, I'd find myself running down a section of trail. I even began to time myself. How different was I, really, from Cave Dog? A competitive spirit is not antithetical to the Long Trail experience. Nor, necessarily, is record seeking. What I realized most profoundly during that summer was how inclusive the Long Trail is—how much room there is for difference, even within one person.

One of the sacred mantras of long-distance hikers is "Hike Your Own Hike," or HYOH. That is, do whatever makes sense to you. Hike barefoot if you want to. Take four days to complete your end-to-end—or fifty years. There are many kinds of hikers in the world, and many ways to get something valuable out of a hike on the Long Trail.

Crossing the Clarendon Gorge suspension bridge.

Hikers head south on the Long Trail from the summit of Mount Abraham.

A DIVERSE CROWD

The trail attracts a diverse crowd — naturalists, vacationers, through-hikers, Vermonters, flatlanders, seekers, those who feel found, tech-weenies with the lightest gear, old-schoolers with packs they've used since the 1960s, families, hunters, school groups, section hikers, day hikers, end-to-enders, women, men, old people and young. Yet commonalities exist among them. For instance, no matter how solitary and contemplative a hiker one is, starting an end-to-end hike at the southern terminus of the Long Trail at the height of summer means interacting with other people. Despite the adamant independence of many hikers, there is a sense of community in the south that is difficult to resist.

The Long Trail and the Appalachian Trail are conjoined twins for the first hundred miles up from the Massachusetts border. The culture of the Appalachian Trail is robust, irrepressible. When I started my

The rushing waters of Clarendon Gorge have cooled the weary feet of many a hiker. Here, Kevin Greszler of Hagerstown, Maryland, takes a break.

end-to-end hike of the Long Trail in the summer of 1997, I was startled to discover that many people didn't use their real names. I met Gray Beard, Blister Free, Ja Love, Cinderella, Hound Dog, Beaujangles, and Joplin—all before Goddard Shelter. We'd leapfrog all day, hiking alone for the most part, but stopping to chat by a river during a rest break. Some of them had been doing that since March in Georgia.

Having shared concerns (the weather, the mileage plan for the day, the weight of one's pack, blisters) breeds a kind of quick honesty. People reveal things they otherwise might not. Getting into a shelter at the end of a fifteen-mile day is different from sharing a ride on a city subway train. You might strike up a conversation in either setting, but a shelter at nightfall is like a truth serum. Over the hiss of a camp stove and the smell of white gas, while hanging wet socks and rubbing sore shoulders, people talk about transitions in their lives, relationships, plans, a desire to defer the complications of their lives for the simplicity of the trail. They also laugh about things that might not seem funny in any other context and talk endlessly about gear, food, mud, and aches and pains. Quiet types might read in a corner and vanish before first light; but there's room for everyone, idiosyncrasies and all. I rarely discovered anyone's given name, and once I continued north after Route 4 and most of the crowd veered eastward to Maine, I never saw or heard from any of them again.

It seems odd now, this lack of lasting connection, but at the time, the relationships were sustaining; they kept us going. They were of a particular moment, and then they were gone.

Young Asa Rosenberg is well protected from the weather as he climbs Mount Elmore (with help).

Opposite, top: A weary backpacker takes a nap beside the Long Trail on Camel's Hump.

Bottom: Participants and instructors in a GMC backpacking workshop enjoy the view from the summit of Camel's Hump.

Of course, it's not just in the south, among Appalachian Trail through-hikers, that one finds a sense of community. The Long Trail attracts people who are curious and people who are generous. End-to-enders often write about "trail magic": moments when the thing they need most seems to miraculously materialize: a cold soda at a trailhead on a sweltering, humid day, a ride into town from a road sparsely traveled—just the right thing at the right moment. And people strike up lasting friendships on the Long Trail.

Still, on an end-to-end hike especially, one notices how things change quite a bit north of Killington. I've gone whole days there without seeing another person on the trail. Shelter logs and end-to-end reports reveal a common thread that I associate with the sections of trail north of the Appalachian Trail, between or beyond the highest peaks, on midweek days, in winter.

FINDING FOCUS IN SOLITUDE

In solitude, people tend to find focus. In *Walking to Vermont*, Christopher Wren says that while walking the trail, "Your outlook on the world gets restricted to rocks, tree roots, puddles, and slick leaves underfoot. The wider reality becomes harder to discern." Walking alone under the weight of a pack can become meditative, can lead to intentness upon each foot falling beyond the next, a falling raindrop, the falling water of the next river, the falling away of all but the present. It's like what an end-to-end hiker that Wren encounters on the trail who goes by the name Stray Cat says when asked why he enjoys hiking:

"'It's a simple life,' Stray Cat supposed, giving more thought to his stove than to my question. 'You don't have to think about anything but hiking and eating.'"

Hiker and friend near Governor Clement Shelter. This hiker's dog is helping with the load, but definitely has the better part of the bargain.

Opposite: Caretakers travel along Mount Mansfield's open summit ridge.

Once, while on a day hike up Mount Abraham on the Battell Trail, I stumbled upon a snake in the treadway that had caught a frog by its leg and was in the process of consuming it. I watched, over the course of an hour, as the snake worked to ingest the frog. The process, which struck me as gruesome at first, became emblematic of the present tense, of paying attention, of focus. People report finding clarity on the trail, feeling more alive. In stopping to witness a process that was akin to birth and death at once, I found myself thoroughly engaged, entirely in that moment. As Dorothy Canfield Fisher says in *Footpath in the Wilderness*, "It is impossible to live the clock around even once, night and day, out under the open sky, without feeling an intimation of greatness, brushing us gently like a huge soft wing, or shaking us to the heart in exaltation." She was onto something: I was out under the open sky for a simple half day of rambling in the woods, and what I found, I ultimately felt, was an intimation of greatness.

GMC member Lexi Shear and daughter Linnaea
at the Hump Brook tent site in Duxbury.

In nature, on the Long Trail, people find poetry. Dorothy Canfield Fisher says, "...it is poetry when you sit on a ledge, silent, watching the shadows lengthen—lengthen, trying to catch the literally infinite gradations of the color, pulsing as it fades. Or when, stirring before dawn, you pause, frying pan in hand perhaps, to gaze, smitten with awe, at the miracle of the daily flooding of our planet with light."

Sometimes the most memorable aspects of a hike are the seemingly least significant, but those that inspire the most poetry. Sure, I remember the day I realized in horror that I'd managed to get turned around and hiked down Worth Mountain immediately after hiking up, adding miles of travel to an already long day. I remember more distinctly, though, that when I finally made it to Boyce Shelter, mist blew through tree branches and the sinking sun set all the rain-covered pine needles aglow, as if every one were draped with golden tinsel.

Stone staircase near Journey's End Camp.

CONSISTENT THEMES

Though people hike on the Long Trail for a million different reasons, I am amazed by the consistency with which certain themes arise. Fisher's observation about poetry in nature was published in 1941. More than fifty years later, Ned Green, a two-time end-to-ender and member of the GMC trail crew who died in an ice-climbing accident in 2001, included this description of "the daily flooding of our planet with light" in an end-to-end report: "Early morning at Glen Ellen...I sit outside my sleeping bag in below-freezing temps and watch the most beautiful sunrise of my hike. There is a low cloud band on the horizon and it is this reddish purple. Intense color. A pillar of pinkish, barely distinguishable light is coming from where the sun is about to rise. A puffy white cloud that is south of the sun is golden. A darker, small cloudbank higher up gets hit with the sun pillar and takes on a purple hue. Now it's time to watch...the sunrise is exquisite, a piece of wonderment as I stare at the blinding orb. I understand why I'm hiking the Long Trail."

Ned Green spent more time on the trail than most people. In his four-day sprint, Cave Dog may not have taken the time for observation, but I'm guessing he felt the poetry of a body maximizing motion. The Long Trail provides a setting for every kind of expression and exertion, for studious observation and forgetting. Maybe that's why so many people form a bond with the trail that lasts a lifetime.

Mansfield caretaker (with friend) relaxes near the summit.

Opposite: Winter sunset atop Camel's Hump.

On my end-to-end hike on the Long Trail, I became more intimately acquainted with Vermont than with any state I've ever chosen as home. On a day hike on Bamforth Ridge in 2007, I began to understand what the Long Trail means to me. It was an evening in July, the decade anniversary of my end-to-end hike. The light was pink-orange and so soft I felt like I was traversing the skin of a peach. I stopped a moment. Nothing stirred. No wind, no footsteps, no voices, no rustling of snakes or chipmunks. The song of a hermit thrush pierced the silence. Plaintive, echoing notes soared and settled in the heavy air; the angled evening light imitated the eloquence of the thrush's song by gilding bright, hardy summer leaves and, at last, giving way to impending darkness. The thrush's song is at once harmonious and dissonant, the layered sounds of solitude and communion, of elation and sorrow; its notes collide and join, clashing and reverberating.

At times I seek solitude on the trail and instead find communion. Sometimes I hike for oblivion, walking as fast as I can until all I notice is rock, root, feet falling rhythmically, heart pounding, and lungs filling with air. Sometimes I stop and will myself to pay attention: to the beauty of a spider's web, the screaming silence of a snowy winter's day, the captivating, complex song of the hermit thrush. The one thing I know about the Long Trail is this: the human hands that created it one hundred years ago reach out and touch those of us who cherish it today, making us all feel that much more connected, that much more alive.

NO TENT CAMPING
CAMP IN SHELTER ONLY

CHAPTER 5

QUIET CONTEMPLATION—AND HARD WORK

The Life of a GMC Shelter Caretaker

BY VAL STORI

At Butler Lodge on the west side of Mount Mansfield, a clear night means a sky full of stars.

IT IS 6:30 A.M. Outside, the birds are stirring—one by one, waking and calling in the predawn light. Turning in my sleeping bag and looking out from my bunk, I see the soft, gray morning light casting the shadow of a mountain ash onto a slab of bedrock outside. Beside me, hikers stir in their sleeping bags, and the rustle of nylon slowly breaks the rhythmic breathing of the night.

My morning ritual begins. As I slip into my clothes beneath the down of my bag, my eyes adjusting to the dim light, I gaze toward the ceiling of the lodge where my eyes rest on the several photos and poems I have tacked in place. "...I find a rock with sun on it / and a stream where the water / runs gentle / and the trees which one by one / give me company..." I am ready for the promises of the day—the gray frosty morning fog, the icy stream, a raven's *kraaww*, a crisp blue sky, and a two-mile commute, on foot, to the summit of Camel's Hump to begin the day's work.

It is late September, and I am spending the fall season as a GMC shelter caretaker at Montclair Glen Lodge on the southern flank of Camel's Hump. I've been here long enough to have settled into a comfortable routine, but I am still appreciative and awed by the subtle changes in light, temperature, and foliage that happen every moment.

I think of the other caretakers waking up on the Long Trail this morning, and I imagine that their experiences are much like mine whether they are waking on the shores of Little Rock Pond or below the summit of Mount Mansfield. I imagine that we are all thankful for the opportunity to live and work among mountains — to rise in the morning amid the energy and expression of the Green Mountains and to hear them speak of unpredictability and truth. For the next several months, our task will be to care for this place — the Long Trail, its shelters, and its fragile alpine summits. We'll also meet and speak to people with different backgrounds and varied mountain experiences. For many, the mountain will present a physical and mental challenge, or perhaps represent a spiritual journey and a significant reminder of one's insignificance amid a greater splendor.

By the time I return from the outhouse (where I have stocked the bark bin and provided discouragement for the lurking spiders), the hikers are in various stages of preparation for the day ahead. The roar of their camp stoves, the creaking of bunks, and the squeaking hinge of the door eliminate the possibility of extra shut-eye. In this small lodge, table space is prime realty, and those who awake late are directed outside to cook their morning meal. Inside, the windows are fogged from the steam rising from piping mugs of coffee and tea. Outside, hikers huddle over the warm vapor of their stoves while waiting for water to boil.

CHANGING STYLES OF CAMP LIFE

In its earlier days, Montclair Glen Lodge, like many of the Long Trail shelters, was furnished with a woodstove. It was a caretaker's responsibility to keep the firewood in supply, and hikers would use the stove to cook their meals and warm their coffee. The depletion of firewood prompted the introduction of kerosene stoves into the back-country by the 1940s. Former GMC caretaker Daan Zwick, who spent the summers of 1939 to 1941 at Taft Lodge, remembers hiking to the Mount Mansfield Summit Hotel several times a summer to pick up five-gallon kerosene cans and hiking them over the ridgeline back to his lodge. While the switch to kerosene lightened his workload of firewood collection, Zwick still cooked his own meals on the woodstove due to the limited availability and expense of kerosene.

Between the 1920s and 1940s, backpackers expected to be able to cook their canned food directly on the shelter's woodstove. Now that

The cliffs of Mount Mansfield's Nose loom high above visitors to the mountain's alpine zone. The summit ridge is Vermont's most extensive area of beautiful and fragile alpine meadows.

A caretaker's responsibilities include educating hikers and others about the need to walk carefully and avoid damage to the fragile plants that live above treeline.

most shelters on the Long Trail have had their woodstoves removed due to the toll of firewood collection on the environment (especially in fragile, subalpine areas), modern hikers are prepared to cook their meals on lightweight backpacking stoves. Last night in the lodge, there was great diversity in the types of stoves and in evening meals. Most meals were one-pot dishes of mac-'n'-cheese, or boil-in-a-bag chicken stew, or dehydrated soup. Living in the lodge, I have the luxury of cooking my meals on a two-burner white gas stove. Often, I fix three-pan meals, but as I near the end of my week in the woods, my supply of fresh vegetables has dwindled, and I, too, am eating dehydrated food products.

This morning, breakfast provides a challenge. After many seasons of caretaking and many bowls of oatmeal and its relatives, I have grown weary of porridge. Yet, peering into my food chest, I see that breakfast porridge seems to be my only choice. Fortunately, lunch preparation is more promising—the usual sandwiches and snacks will provide welcome fuel for the tough hike and work ahead. The days I'm out doing trail work, I get hungry from the physical labor, and the days I'm caretaking on the summit, I get hungry simply trying to stay warm! Summit caretaking involves spending hours on Vermont's alpine peaks in both sunny and inclement weather talking with hikers about the fragility of the alpine tundra. Often, the views are rewarding, the breeze slight, and the sunshine illimitable. Just as often, however, the weather is ominous and temperatures hover in the 50-degree range. With any luck, while on summit duty I will meet a camp or school group, college outing club, or grandmother-type who will offer up a cookie or home-baked goody. I shall never forget the piping-hot mug of cider offered to me on a windy and frigid October day that raised my spirits and warmed my core.

In this photograph, three summit caretakers on Mount Mansfield take a break with a canine companion. From left are Roderick Rice, Al Donovan, and Daan Zwick. The photo dates from the 1930s or early 1940s.

CARETAKERS OF SEASONS PAST

Caretakers have not always been the recipients of such delicacies. In fact, when the caretaker program first began in 1920, it was the caretakers who were providing the treats to weary hikers. While I usually had plenty of hot tea and conversation to share at Montclair Glen Lodge, I've never proffered soda or blankets to my guests. But from my conversations with Daan Zwick, I learned that in the past, caretakers packed such things up to their cabins to sell to hikers. When Zwick was caretaking in the 1930s, a caretaker's salary was the revenue generated from overnight fees (often ranging from twenty to fifty dollars a summer), so for supplementary income, caretakers would sell goods and meals to hikers. The overnight fee was fifty cents and included a blanket and mattress. For an additional sum, Zwick would offer hikers a soda (chilling in the stream behind Taft Lodge) or a specialty meal such as creamed dried beef and peas with a slice of freshly baked pie straight from the chimney oven on the woodstove. I can imagine the inviting warmth of the lodge after a wet and tiring day of hiking and working on the Long Trail and the ensuing satisfaction of a hearty meal.

The first caretakers on the Long Trail were hired and managed by Burlington Section volunteers. The section initially stationed caretakers at Butler and Taft Lodge on Mount Mansfield and hired young men (high school or college level) to fill the positions. Shortly thereafter, the GMC hired caretakers at Griffith Lake, Killington Peak, Camel's Hump, and the Long Trail Lodge. These caretakers were responsible for firewood collection, trail clearing, and shelter upkeep.

A caretaker packs in tools for summer trail maintenance.

By the time Daan Zwick became caretaker at Taylor Lodge in the summer of 1938, not much had changed. Zwick's salary was based on his fee collections, and due to the "remoteness" of the lodge, he earned twenty dollars that quiet summer. It was so quiet that he also managed to read Shakespeare's complete works. He fared better at Taft in the summer of 1939, where the bunk space for thirty-four people attracted constant traffic from end-to-enders, summer campers, and weekenders. The following year at Taft Lodge, Zwick was given his first official salary of seventy-five dollars for the entire summer season, which ran from late June through Labor Day weekend. For two months each summer, he busied himself by gathering firewood, collecting water, and packing kerosene. In addition, he cleared winter blowdowns from all the trails within a two-mile radius. Not surprisingly, he learned how to use a two-man saw!

I imagine that Zwick's hikes across the pristine Mansfield ridgeline (there were no towers in those days), while weighted by jugs of kerosene, were in many ways similar to the sublime experiences of modern caretakers who cross the ridgeline in the early morning or evening after a day of work. At these quiet and solitary hours, the mountain belongs to the song of the Bicknell's thrush, the trill of the junco, and the chill of a northwestern wind. Like all caretakers, Zwick remembers these transcendent moments and recalls the mornings when the valley below Mansfield was enshrouded in morning fog and the Presidential range was silhouetted by the rising sun.

Opposite, top: Jeanne Joudry looks out from the Stratton Mountain fire tower on a windy day.

Bottom: Sunlight streams through Taft Lodge windows.

GREEN MOUNTAIN
CLUB
THE LONG TRAIL
VERMONT

A view of Lincoln Mountain on a misty fall day photographed by Senator Patrick Leahy from his family's farm in Middlesex. Senator Leahy has helped obtain significant federal funding for Long Trail land protection.

Caretaker Tim Sullivan keeping an eye on the weather atop Camel's Hump.

CHANGING CARETAKER DUTIES

Today, caretakers face a variety of duties, which can include site maintenance, trail maintenance, backcountry education, backcountry sanitation, and alpine summit duty. Some caretakers work at shelters while others work at backcountry campsites or on alpine summits.

A less pleasurable part of caretakers' duties: turning outhouse compost.

The goal of the caretaker program has shifted from providing fuel wood or kerosene for hikers to protecting the natural resources of the Long Trail. Yet, despite this shift in backcountry management, the caretaker program always has attracted young, idealistic men and women in search of simplicity. This important change in management aims began in the 1960s with the start of the summit stewardship program, then called the Ranger-Naturalist Program. The hiking boom of the mid-1970s precipitated the expansion of the caretaker program. Because of the increased use they were seeing, it became necessary to include more caretakers at shelters and campsites.

In the late 1970s, the program focused on minimizing the effects of backcountry recreation through education and on-site management. Today, the summit caretaker program provides education and information about the fragility of alpine plants and stresses the importance of Leave No Trace backcountry ethics. Additionally, the GMC introduced batch-bin composting toilets to overnight sites on the Long Trail and began replacing its pit privies at all its high-use sites. Today, a caretaker's workload includes turning and drying the waste pile and carrying loads of bark mulch to the privy.

QUIET MOMENTS

Back to basics: With no television, no phones, and no electricity, most caretakers find simpler ways to pass the time.

Opposite: Despite frequent visitors, sometimes a caretaker may find solitude on the summit of Camel's Hump.

With all the work to be done both on the trail and at the site, one might wonder how a caretaker gets any off-duty time. In the course of a season, each caretaker develops a rhythm and routine. Early risers often slip into the woods for morning yoga or journal reflections; night owls often lie out under the stars or take moonlight jaunts. To catch the sun setting over the Adirondacks or the moon rising over the Whites, caretakers often linger on the summits long after the hikers have descended. Each has her special nooks and crannies, her favorite haunts to sit with nature, play her flute, or capture the golden afternoon glow with paints or pastels. It is these private moments amidst the sublime beauty of the Long Trail coupled with the simplicity of life in the woods that draws people to the caretaker program time and time again. Zwick, for example, spent four seasons as a caretaker and still fondly recalls the morning song of the white-throated sparrow and the pure mountain water he drank straight from the stream.

In the long line of GMC caretakers, the prevailing sentiment is one of gratitude for the ability to live simply in the unspoiled Vermont woods. Most have enrolled in the caretaker program with a strong sense of idealism and a passion for the simple life.

Since the 1920s, the caretaker program has provided caretakers not only an opportunity to live close to nature, but also an opportunity to interact with hikers of different interests, abilities, and ages. Peg Whitson, caretaker at Bolton Lodge in 1975, reflects that after a summer of both hard physical labor and complete relaxation, she "has renewed faith in the human race…I have served my guests well…I have learned to be generous with what I have. I've given food, stove, candles, and time. I have received in return more food, money, fuel, and best of all, much good will."

On my return to Montclair Glen Lodge after an afternoon on the summit of Camel's Hump, I think about the evening before me. I am sure that there will be plenty of guests in the lodge tonight, and I am looking forward to their hearty conversation and the warmth of the lodge. But now the woods are quiet and the sweet smell of autumn hangs in the air. As I cross through Wind Gap, I hear a bull moose's deep-throated grunt in the distance. A cacophony of chickadees ensues. I walk slowly this last quarter mile, etching the fall scene permanently into my memory.

A CARETAKER'S LIFE

PHOTO ESSAY BY ALDEN PELLETT

Above: A sign politely informs visitors they have a role in protecting the summit vegetation.

Right: Caretaker Robin Lenner.

Green Mountain Club summit caretaker Robin Lenner spent the fall of 2007 near the top of Mount Mansfield, tending Butler Lodge and watching over the fragile alpine zone of Mansfield's summit ridge. Her days were filled with activity, and her responsibilities ranged from educating hikers to turning compost from the lodge's outhouse. She returned to her mountainside cabin each night, tired and ready for a simple meal and sleep.

Fortunately, the work was outdoors, in one of the Northeast's most beautiful places. Every job has its benefits!

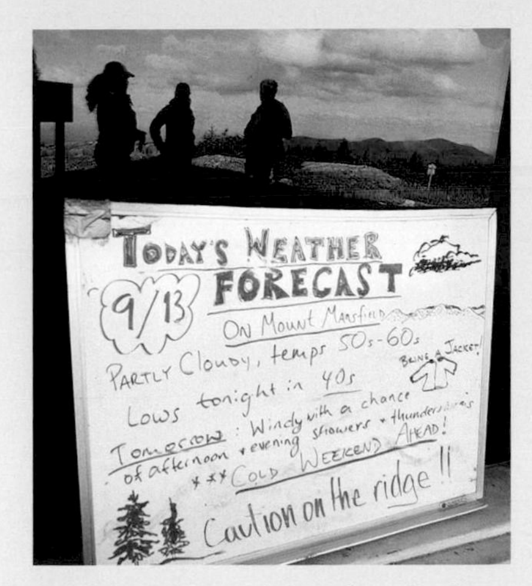

From left: At the top of the Toll Road, information for visitors; Robin turning compost; checking on the outhouse collector.

Climbing the Wampahoofus Trail to the summit; along the Forehead Bypass Trail.

Evening at Butler Lodge: Cooking supper, entries in the journal, and, then, to bed.

CHAPTER 6

THE TRAILKEEPERS

The Mud and Sweat of Trail Work

BY VAL STORI

IN 1931, the Green Mountain Club's board of directors authorized the formation of a paid crew to construct and maintain the treadway and the overnight camps of the Long Trail. Thus was born the first Long Trail Patrol (LTP), a small crew of young men who dedicated their summers to clearing and maintaining the remote northern sections of the Long Trail.

Today, the GMC oversees three trail crews: two paid LTPs and one volunteer LTP. While the club still strives to provide a simple footpath through the wilderness, a century of change has somewhat modified the type of work that the LTP undertakes. Much of the work has remained the same, but advances in technology have altered how the work is done and the materials used. In addition, the composition and daily routine of the patrol have changed.

Ever wonder why that trail is passable? Trail crews like this one on Belvidere Mountain make all the difference.

It was also 1931 when the GMC hired a retired electrical engineer named Roy Buchanan as the LTP's first leader. In time, Buchanan became a legendary figure in the GMC; even after his retirement from the LTP in 1967, he remained a vibrant volunteer. Consequently, much of the history of the LTP is inexorably linked with the life and passion of Roy Buchanan. Buchanan's affable personality, woodsman's knowledge, and resourceful efficiency were perfect for the job; many young men who returned for several summers to work on the LTP recalled Buchanan's penchant for storytelling and his good sense of humor. They also recalled his wife Helen's homemade doughnuts, which helped keep crew spirits high!

In its earlier days, the members of the LTP began each summer by clearing blowdowns and brush from the trail—mostly north of Route 15, where volunteers rarely ventured and sections did not patrol. This work progressed slowly because of limited access to the remote northern sections of the trail and the limited speed of axes and crosscut saws.

In this photo from the 1930s, Roy Buchanan sits on the running board of Patrol Truck No. 1 with two crew members close at hand.

At the start of each week, the young men (there were no women on the patrol at that time) would gather at Buchanan's home in Burlington where they would pack the canvas-backed Chevrolet pickup with tools, camping equipment, food (including Helen's doughnuts), and wooden pack frames and set off for the trailhead. At the end of each workday, the crew would pile into the truck and head to Barrows Camp, a frame building erected in 1931 near Route 15 and the village of Johnson that was used until 1994 when it was replaced by Roundtop Shelter. On the return to Barrows each night, the crew would stop at the nearby Washer Farm for fresh milk and eggs. Dinner was a communal affair, with all the food provided by the GMC. Crew members would take turns cooking the meals on Coleman gas stoves.

The latter half of crew summers would be spent repairing and constructing shelters on the Long Trail—resulting in what have become known as the "Buchanan-style" Long Trail shelters such as Tillotson Camp, Journey's End Camp, and Ritterbush Camp. These characteristic camps (which were based on the logging camps of the time) were relatively easy to build and also used space efficiently. Classic Buchanan-style camps were quite small, generally designed to sleep six hikers. Many of them have succumbed to the ravages of time and no longer exist. One, Journey's End Camp, has been moved to the GMC campus in Waterbury Center.

The interior of each cabin contained two sets of bunks separated by a table in the middle. The elongated bunk platforms would serve as benches for the table. The front third of the cabin remained as open floor space for backpacks and the like—and sometimes hosted a woodstove. Butler Lodge on Mount Mansfield, the largest of the camps Buchanan built, would sleep fourteen hikers, and was said to be the one he was most proud of. In all, Buchanan and his crews added thirty-seven camps and shelters to the Long Trail.

Long Trail Patrol members Paul Pearce and Jonas Kurtz prepare to move a large rock to a more advantageous spot.

FOREST CONSTRUCTION TECHNIQUES

Harris Abbott, LTP member from 1957 to 1961, recalls working with Buchanan on Whiteface Shelter, Butler Lodge, Emily Proctor Shelter, Pico Camp, and Cooper Lodge. On some (fortunate) occasions, boards for bunks or siding would be skidded up old logging roads by horses pulling stone boats. But Abbott recalls that in the late 1950s and 1960s, when replacing shelters, spruce trees would be felled and peeled in the nearby forest and then skidded by hand to the construction site. When rebuilding a shelter, crew members would salvage all possible materials such as metal roofing and nails, rather than haul up new supplies. Since shelter reconstruction usually took two to three

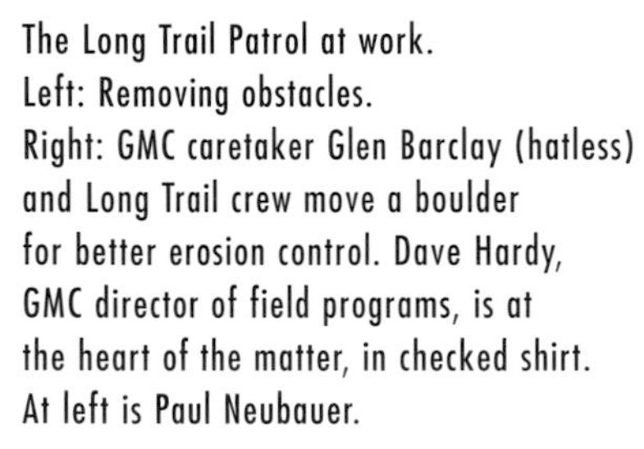

The Long Trail Patrol at work.
Left: Removing obstacles.
Right: GMC caretaker Glen Barclay (hatless) and Long Trail crew move a boulder for better erosion control. Dave Hardy, GMC director of field programs, is at the heart of the matter, in checked shirt. At left is Paul Neubauer.

weeks, the crew would sleep in a temporary shelter made from the old metal roofing. Spruce boughs from the newly cut trees made soft, aromatic sleeping mats.

Weight-saving techniques included using a metal pie pan with a small amount of water covering the bottom as a level and constructing bunks out of hardware cloth (wire mesh) nailed between the stringers, instead of milled lumber. Ironically, such painstaking efforts to reduce the amount of material carried into the backcountry were overshadowed by the monumental effort it took to equip shelters with woodstoves, which occasionally had to be packed in or carried long distances. Fortunately for Abbott, the woodstove that he helped carry into Taft Lodge in the 1960s made its journey up Mount Mansfield via the auto road. Unfortunately for Abbott, the woodstove then had to be packed across the ridgeline and down the Profanity Trail—all in one piece!

Nearly fifty years later, Abbott laughs as he recounts the challenging adventure: "Later, when we were making extensive renovations to the lodge—replacing several logs that had rotted out on the south end, rebuilding bunks, and the like—most of the supplies had been brought over from the new gondola, except for the woodstove—that was driven up the auto road. I thought I had it relatively easy until it came time to descend via the Profanity Trail. It was steep back then, too—and aptly named."

Top: LTP member Eric Evans often worked in his kilt; Bottom: Outhouse instruction.

BACKWOODS HUMOR

And of course, along with shelters came privies—a prime place for Buchanan and his crews to exercise their sense of humor. Few of us likely remember the first Battell Shelter privy—an enclosed log structure so large that it was nicknamed Battell Lodge. Its current successor pays tribute to the former privy in size and grandeur.

Buchanan's son Chet (also an electrical engineer), who joined the patrol for several summers, gravitated toward building and naming privies. The duo "christened" several of these with names such as the Whiteface Observatory and the Defecatorium. But the laughs did not stop there—the electrical engineers painted an ammeter on the seat of a privy with the needle on full discharge.

A week in the woods with little diversion invariably leads to comic creativity and laissez-faire attitudes. Such was the case on the day in 2005 when the concrete arrived for the tower abutments on the Lamoille River bridge project. Instead of driving several miles to the other side of the river and hiking one and a half miles to the abutment site, crew members decided to save time and energy by stripping off their clothes and swimming to the other side. Fully expecting their clothes and shoes to be ferried across the highline, the crew members were surprised to find that the first tub slid across the highline contained ready-to-pour concrete—not clothing. It was reported that no one suffered from sunburn or poison ivy.

It is precisely such humor, dedication, and expertise that have contributed to the success and longevity of the GMC's LTP. The LTP program continues to set the standard for professional, innovative, and enduring trail work. For example, the original cost estimate provided by consulting engineers for the Lamoille River bridge project mentioned above was $360,000 But GMC staff and volunteers built the bridge for less than half that original estimate.

On steeper sections of the Long Trail system, the LTP has designed and installed features to protect the treadway. For example, in 2006 the crew pinned wooden ladders flush to the exposed bedrock, backfilling the rungs with crushed rock on the upper reaches of the Hedgehog Brook Trail. In more exposed areas, the LTP has pinned rock or log steps into the bedrock with rebar and epoxy.

Beginning in the 1970s, in response to the hiking boom (and the steep grade of much of the Long Trail), heavy trail construction became the focus of the LTP. Today, crew work primarily focuses on "hardening the treadway" by installing rock structures such as water bars and stairs, which arrest erosion and minimize the gullying of trails in steep terrain. Such "rock work" is a slow and consequently expensive endeavor, but the GMC and its partners are committed to funding and supporting the restoration of the Long Trail and its side trails.

While the crews are no longer hauling woodstoves into the backcountry, they are hauling in eighteen-pound steel rock bars, grip hoists, rock drills, sledgehammers, and a week's worth of food and overnight supplies—which are all necessary for moving and setting rocks in the treadway. Given the remote nature of the upper reaches of the Long Trail, crews now spend the entire work week living in the woods in "spike camps" of several tents stealthily set up off the trail. And because of the narrow trail corridor, the slow regeneration of natural resources, and the development of backcountry ethics, the crews no longer sleep on spruce boughs.

The Thundering Falls handicapped-accessible trail in Killington, under construction in 2007.

At the start of the work week, crews of five to ten people each load trucks with gear, food, and tools and set off for the trailhead. Unfortunately, Patrol Truck No. 1 is long gone, but it has been replaced by other, equally loved (and equally vintage) trucks such as "Joe," the 1979 GMC Sierra, and "Dakota," the 1986 red Dodge Dakota.

Most of the first day is spent packing in supplies and setting up the spike camp. The site of the camp is chosen well in advance of the crew season and takes into consideration principles of backcountry ethics and ways of minimizing impact on vegetation and soil. Crews no longer have the luxury of living in Barrows Camp and enjoying farm fresh milk each morning. Instead, the crews not only must work in whatever weather the skies provide, but also must lie down and sleep in it too. Yet the spirited young men and women who sign up seem to seek such conditions. Despite the adversity of a season of life and work outdoors, they thrive and build strong bonds with each other and with the Long Trail.

RECENT MAJOR PROJECTS

Recently, the LTP undertook several major technical projects that expanded the scope of its work. Two recent examples are the Thundering Falls handicapped-accessible trail in Killington and the Lamoille suspension bridge. Both projects required expertise, innovative design, significant funding, and years of work.

The Lamoille suspension bridge, a major accomplishment of the Long Trail Patrol, took two years to complete and was finished in 2005. Below: A section of the bridge plans.

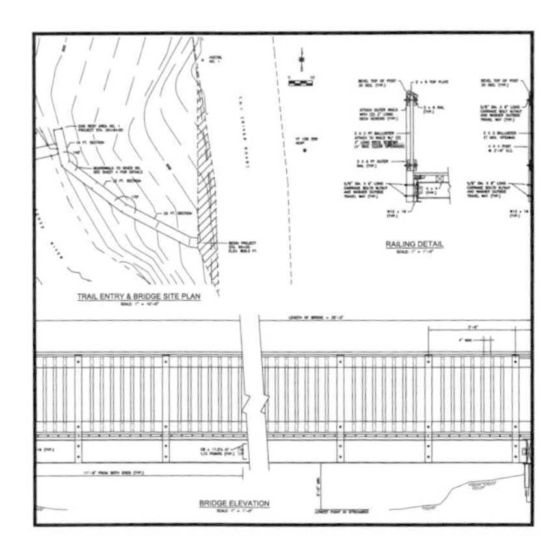

The Thundering Falls (2005–2008) project, which involved relocating nearly half a mile of trail across the Ottauquechee River and its floodplain, became one of the GMC's most challenging endeavors. The project entailed setting sixty-foot steel piers with a hydraulic driver through the muck and into solid ground below. Kelly Walsh recalled, "The piers came with extenders, in five- and seven-foot lengths; if the pier did not meet the proper resistance once it was driven in, we'd have to attach extenders — at times to a depth of eighty feet!"

Atop the piers, the LTP constructed a wheelchair-accessible boardwalk out of lumber framing and fabricated decking. Director of field programs Dave Hardy, who described the project as "the project that ate our field seasons," added that, "the GMC is proud to have constructed this flagship boardwalk to one of the most beautiful waterfalls in Vermont."

The Lamoille suspension bridge took the LTP two years to complete (2004–2005). The 136-foot suspension bridge over the Lamoille River relocates the Long Trail near Route 15. The project provided an exciting learning experience for the trail crew and Greg Western, former GMC field supervisor. Western said the bridge project represented a

century of knowledge about working with hand tools, using ingenuity and creativity to build to twenty-first-century load regulations and standards without compromising on the GMC's wilderness values or the way the club has always done things.

"We were given the engineering specs, and then we were faced with our resources—people power, ingenuity, and a block and tackle," he said. "Just how do you stand up a thirty-foot steel post onto bolts without a crane? And how do you get all the materials to the other side of the river without road access?"

That was the LTP's challenge; once accomplished, it became its greatest feat. As a group, members of the LTP generated ideas for assembling the bridge and set about fabricating custom pieces to transport bridge materials. In the end, the bridge parts were cabled across the river with a block and tackle. The mixed concrete was transported across a highline in tubs custom-made by volunteer Al Fiebig, and the thirty-foot posts were hoisted into the air using a homemade pole with a scribed bracket.

Lunch on a trail crew is not always elegant.

Opposite: Butler Lodge, one of the oldest and most popular of the GMC lodges, was originally constructed by Roy Buchanan and others in 1933. Here, in July 2000, the lodge undergoes a major rebuilding.

RESTORING SHELTERS

Although trail construction and repair constitute the lion's share of crew projects, the LTP still plays an important role in the restoration of Long Trail shelters. Several of the eighty shelters on the Long Trail are in need of restoration each year. While volunteers often play a larger role in the construction and restoration of shelters, in remote and unpopulated areas, the work is assigned to paid patrol crews. Some shelters, such as Rolston Rest, need to be completely torn down and rebuilt; others, such as William B. Douglas Shelter or Tillotson Camp, require renovation. In either case, if a shelter is more than fifty years old, it is eligible for the National Register of Historic Places and requires the GMC to obtain permits from the Vermont Division of Historic Preservation. With such permission, the GMC may restore or rebuild the shelter to standards developed by the state. This level of protection ensures that the Buchanan-style shelter (and other historic styles) will endure.

Although shelter styles may stand the test of time, some elements of the old-fashioned construction methods have changed. Gone are the days of cutting and peeling logs on-site and of hardware cloth bunks. Today, most materials for shelter repair and construction are brought in by helicopter. Nails, roofing, privies, logs and lumber, generators, electric saws, and nail guns are flown in with relative ease and precision. The crews then work closely with volunteers to notch and assemble replacement logs, restore interiors, and replace windows. This was the case of the Peru Peak Shelter renovation in the summer of 2000. The LTP rebuilt the 1933 Civilian Conservation Corps shelter, retaining the original footprint and style of the former shelter. Crew members worked closely with staff from the Green Mountain National Forest to coordinate the helicopter drop.

However, in designated wilderness areas, flying materials onto the Long Trail is prohibited. In the case of the Emily Proctor Shelter reconstruction in 2002, located in the Breadloaf Wilderness, the LTP was faced with the tough choice of harvesting trees on-site or hauling in lumber for the shelter, privy, and tent platforms. And thus, after much discussion, the crew carried the lumber via the rocky and steady ascent of the 3.5-mile-long Emily Proctor Trail.

Trail crew members.

A BOND CREATED

The next one hundred years are sure to bring new challenges and changes to the LTP, but some things are just as likely to remain the same. The Long Trail will always remain a simple footpath in the wilderness, and as such, it will continue to attract adventurous young people seeking an opportunity to live and work in the woods. The crews will always invest their love for the out of doors, their sweat, and their ingenuity in the trail.

And whether it is Helen's homemade doughnuts or a week of working in the rain, LTP members take with them fond memories of their time on the trail. Former LTP leader Kelly Walsh recalled that her summer on the LTP was a time of hard physical labor and convivial camaraderie. "The bond you create with your crew members is unique. Living, sweating, eating, and sharing days off with the same group of people is an intense work environment, but amazing friendships are always created," Walsh said. "This is especially true of young women. We get such a boost in self-confidence with this kind of work. It's fabulous to see young women become more confident as they thrive in this environment."

Harris Abbott, who worked with Roy Buchanan and others in the 1950s and 1960s, agrees with Walsh's sentiment. "I will always look back on my days as a Long Trail Patrol member with fondness," he said.

This team of horses helped bring construction materials in to Lost Pond Shelter.

VOLUNTEERING: A GMC TRADITION

In 2006, volunteer Scott Christiansen (with the help of some field staff) packed a 100-pound generator up the Cliff Trail on Mount Mansfield and used it to insert steel rod handholds into the cliffs of one of the highest and most exposed locations on the Long Trail system. Armed with the generator, a rock drill, and epoxy, he exemplified the commitment and devotion (call it extremism if you will) that is typical of Long Trail volunteers.

Not all volunteers manifest their love for the Long Trail by carrying heavy equipment up cliffs, yet all have given much of themselves to assist in the GMC's mission to "make the Vermont Mountains play a larger part in the life of the people by protecting and maintaining the Long Trail System." Together, from the volunteers who paint blazes to volunteers like Christiansen, they have accomplished the Herculean feat of developing and maintaining the Long Trail and its many side trails since its inception in 1910.

From the beginning, through the formation of sections, the GMC has depended on volunteers in all of its endeavors. For its first twenty years, it operated as an exclusively volunteer organization, and it was not until 1977 that it hired its first executive director. In the early years, the first chapter, the Mount Mansfield Section, cleared the trail from Sterling Pond to Camel's Hump in just two years — without a penny of remuneration. Since then, thirteen other chapters have formed, and they have continued the tradition of lending their blood, their sweat, and occasionally their tears to the ongoing task of clearing (and reclearing) trail and to building (and rebuilding) shelters — sometimes with the help of the LTP and sometimes without. Over the years, as sections emerged and withered away, trail duties were reassigned and energetic new volunteers were found.

Basil Goodridge working on Buchanan Lodge in 1984.

Shelter reconstruction efforts, charismatic leaders, or inspirational outings often proved to be the driving forces behind the revitalization of waning sections. The Sterling Section, for example, came together in 1911 to cut the trail north of Smugglers' Notch to Johnson, and it rallied in the 1930s around the construction of several Long Trail shelters such as French and Barrows Camps. However, in time the section dwindled to a few members and gradually disappeared.

Eventually, Henry Mould, through his efforts to construct a replacement shelter for the dilapidated Mould Lodge in Beaver Meadow, sparked the revival of the section. Beginning in the spring of 1947, volunteers from the Sterling Section turned up every Sunday to erect a new log cabin at Beaver Meadow, in the shadow of Morse, Whiteface, and Madonna Mountains. The logs were cut and peeled in the vicinity, and a horse was used to skid the logs into place. The rest of the materials (including the stove) were carried 2.5 miles from the nearest road. It was a labor-intensive process that drew people from their homes and brought them together to work as a team, and the section was reborn.

William Sanders, in his *Beaver Meadow Lodge History*, wrote, "During the building the cows went un-milked, loved ones were forgotten, fish poles, hitherto in constant use, stood in the closet gathering cobwebs...fingernails were pounded, several new cuss-words were coined...Thus have the works of nature and man been blended into these pleasant surroundings..."

Being a volunteer on the Long Trail does not mean that you must carry the equivalent of three-fourths of your body weight up a mountainside in a pack or shirk your family duties. In fact, GMC leaders want volunteers to bring their families with them on volunteer outings. One volunteer who has done just this is Marge Fish. In 1976, shortly after having moved to Vermont, she read an announcement in the local paper that the Killington Section was hosting a work day. An avid hiker and a newlywed, Marge sweet-talked her husband, Bob, into attending a waterbar-cleaning outing, and a long, fruitful marriage between the young couple and the trail was born. Even the birth of their two children did not keep them from the trail. Instead, Bob and Marge Fish became shelter adopters for Peru Peak Shelter and later Big Branch Shelter, which proved to be the perfect distance from the trailhead for coaxing young children into making shelter maintenance visits.

Eric Seidel at work on Bamforth Ridge Shelter.

Thirty years later, Fish no longer needs M&Ms to lure her offspring into the woods step by step. Both her children are active volunteers—not only on the Long Trail, but also in other local organizations. "It became a lifestyle for our entire family," said Fish. "The woods became an important place for us to gather as a family and for me to refill my personal wealth. With the Long Trail so close to our home, we felt that we needed to give back to the trail. Our family has made such strong ties with the trail and the other volunteers we've met—now we want to make sure that the trail lasts for future generations."

Fish's sentiment is echoed by many Long Trail volunteers. Jean Haigh, charter member of the Northeast Kingdom Section, has been an active volunteer with the GMC for the last eight years. In 2005, Haigh helped restore the old fire tower on Vermont's Monadnock Mountain. She recalls a 90-degree June day when more than eighty people congregated in the small town of Lemington to haul 180 pieces of lumber up the 3,148-foot mountain. Despite the heat and voracious black flies, Haigh recalls the challenging work day with enthusiasm. "My emphasis has been to get more people involved with the trails in the kingdom," Haigh said. "Seeing so many folks show up to take part in hands-on work was, for me, fuel for continuing my efforts at protecting the longevity of the Long Trail and now the NEK trails." She added that her volunteer efforts have helped her meet many people who share her values and her love of the outdoors. "I've made good friends," she added, "and now I always have folks to hike with!"

The late Tom Abbott at work building the new Laura Woodward Shelter in 2001. Abbot passed away just days after completing work on Rolston Rest in 2004.

LIFELONG VOLUNTEERING

For many GMCers, Long Trail volunteerism has been a lifelong commitment. Most of them have embodied a love of the outdoors and a passion for trail work. Gardiner Lane moved to Vermont in 1969 and became an active volunteer with the Burlington Section, maintaining the Long Trail between Johnson and Bolton. He loved clearing trail, and he loved the camaraderie and humor he found while working with friends on the Long Trail. His longtime friend Clem Holden recalled, "When I became seventy-eight, and Gardiner was ten years older than me, I said to Leo Leach [of the Burlington Section], 'I think you better pull us off; Roy Buchanan quit at seventy-eight.' Leach replied, 'Did you ask Gardiner?' I did that and Gardiner said, 'No way.' He wanted to keep going, right up to the end."

And there are many others who share the same sentiment and life-long commitment. Take Jack Harrington for example, who in his seventies spent several weekends working on the new Bamforth Ridge Shelter—work that included climbing onto the top of the shelter to nail down the roof boards.

Ottaquechee Section member Don Whitney took his first hike up Pico Peak as a ten-year-old; in 1977, he began working on the trail, and after his retirement in 1987, he began devoting much of his time to trail work. The major project at the time was the relocation of the Appalachian Trail near Pico onto a permanently protected corridor. "My most memorable trail accomplishment was the work I did with other section members to build the new stretch of trail. It was not like digging waterbars," Whitney recounted. "It was quite a challenge, and we did a lot ourselves, including the route layout and the rough cutting." While Whitney no longer hikes miles into the woods, he still loves being outdoors and volunteering for the GMC. Today, he recruits and trains volunteers to monitor the corridor boundary of the trail he helped build. In this manner, Whitney passes on his enthusiasm for the trail.

Leah Burdick finishing the job at the Hump Brook Tenting Area.

The trail is sustained by a long list of impressive volunteers of all ages and skills. Some volunteers bring construction expertise and are instrumental in designing and framing some of the most beautiful shelters on the Long Trail, while others bring their youthful spirit and dedication to community service. Erik and Laurel Tobiason, timber framers from Barnard, Vermont, have designed several signature post-and-beam shelters such as Bromley Shelter. Other volunteers, including Eagle Scouts from the Boy Scouts of America (BSA), engage in projects on the Long Trail that emphasize the BSA philosophy of learning by doing, service to others, and good citizenship. Eagle Scouts have built composting privies, cleaned waterbars, installed rock staircases, and hauled supplies for shelter construction.

YOUNG TRAIL AND SHELTER WORKERS

Increasingly, camp, college, and school groups have been giving back to the Long Trail by donating their invaluable labor to the GMC. Often, these young, strong groups will assist GMC staff and volunteers in hands-on trail work or shelter construction. In 2006, a group of volunteers from Burr and Burton Academy worked with Marge Fish to carry in 325 pounds of coal, 1.5 cubic feet of stone, a fifty-five-gallon plastic drum, and other materials to the Stratton Pond Shelter for the construction of a new composting system.

Fish likes to find opportunities to work with young people on the trail. She firmly believes in getting kids outdoors and helping them discover the magical, "ah-ha" moments on the trail. "Recently," she

At the end of the day, the ridges and ranges of the Green Mountains gather mist.

recalled, laughing, "I was working on the trail with three girls from the Burr and Burton Academy Outing Club. We came across some blowdowns, but the girls were reluctant to use the bow saw, claiming that 'girls can't cut blowdowns.' Well, after a little coaxing, the girls cleared the trail all the way from the summit of Bromley to the new shelter, and let me tell you, they loved every minute of it and impressed themselves with their newfound 'girl power.'"

Volunteer time on the Long Trail can also be a solo experience. Trail and shelter adopters often work by themselves in their thrice-annual maintenance visits. Solo trail work experience is multifaceted: it can be a test of physical strength and endurance, a time for reflection, and a time for bonding with the trail. Little mishaps can become humbling and educational experiences; after pinching a saw and hiking back to the car to retrieve your ax, you quickly learn to release the tension in a blowdown before making the cut.

Through the years, Heinz Trebitz, an Ottauquechee section member and trail adopter, learned many new tricks by trial and tribulation

and by working with experienced volunteers. Fifteen years later, Trebitz is intimately familiar with the two miles of Appalachian Trail that he maintains. "I know every fallen tree that I've removed, every water bar I've cleaned over and over again. When you maintain a trail and work on it, it becomes a part of you," Trebitz said.

◆

All volunteers walk away with a part of the Long Trail etched into memory. Many are thankful for the Long Trail as a footpath, as a symbol of cooperative spirit, and as a place for connecting with the Green Mountains. They happily give of their time and labor to perpetuate the trail's magic, and the Green Mountain Club could not accomplish all it has without their efforts. In return, as volunteers share the work and as they share stories and personal experiences, the social fabric of the GMC is woven, good friends are made, and the Long Trail is given a strong future as both a natural resource and a community builder.

CHAPTER 7

THE NATURAL WORLD

Of Deep Forests, a Tiny Mushroom, and Bicknell's Thrush

BY BRYAN PFEIFFER

These stately maples are typical of the deciduous forests that blanket the lower elevations of Vermont's Green Mountains.

FROM THE SUMMIT of Mount Grant, the nature of the Long Trail unfolds at a hiker's feet. This lofty spot (3,623 feet above sea level) is about halfway between Massachusetts and Canada. Yet it boasts no particular celebrated status on the trail, unless, of course, you believe each step along this route is itself a celebration. In any case, Mount Grant is a fine spot to stop and ponder the diversity of life on the spine of Vermont—whatever flies, flutters, darts, jumps, scampers, walks, crawls, slithers, swims, grows, decays, or even only sits there beside this illustrious path.

Visible far to the south of Mount Grant is some of the Long Trail's more gentle terrain, a high plateau where a hiker can swim in remote ponds and circumnavigate mysterious bogs. Southern trees and unusual plants, at least by Green Mountain standards, like bitternut hickory and Goldie's fern, sprout here and there in a few locations. And hikers in June might find early hairstreak—a prize butterfly about the size of your thumbnail, colored in shocking cobalt blue and mint green marked with little orange lightning bolts.

Somewhere off in the distance to the north are the trail's classic and most recognizable peaks. As hikers here walk atop Vermont, they pass tiny flowering plants more typical of the Arctic than New England. And if that isn't

View from the summit of Mount Abraham in winter.

Yet over the course of several hundred million years after their formation, much of the Grenville Mountains eroded away. As they eroded, continental plates began to separate, resulting in a new ocean. The sediments and deceased marine life that accumulated in that ocean would go on to become the raw materials for the next round of mountain building, which took place about 450 million years ago. Known as the Taconic Orogeny, this event was monumental in the evolution of the Long Trail. As plates moved together again, ocean sediments and crusts were forced skyward and went on to become much of what is now the Green Mountains. An additional orogeny about 360 million years ago, the Acadian Orogeny, would further deform and uplift these mountains, but the Taconic Orogeny would truly lay the foundation for a footpath to come millions of years later. So although we lump them together as "the Green Mountains," the range actually results from a series of orogenies, each with its own blend of rock formations, occurring hundreds of millions of years apart. The bedrock diversity can lend diversity to the nature of the trail itself because a given rock type, as we shall see, tends to support its own community of plants and animals.

But orogenies did not end the formation of the Long Trail's character. If the monumental collision of oceanic and continental plates hundreds of millions of years ago gave rise to a rough-and-ready mountainous landscape, the advance and retreat of glaciers added the finishing touches.

For the last two to three million years, ice sheets have repeatedly advanced and retreated across northern parts of North America, redefining our landscape many times. But the most recent march of ice (to as far south as Long Island) made the Green Mountains much of what they are today. It is important to note that glaciers are much more than ice. They are an amalgam of ice, rock, and sediments, anything the advancing glacier had scraped up along its path. This advancing heap eradicates whatever animals, plants, fungi and other organisms cannot get out of the way. The glaciers generally advanced from the north-northwest toward the south-southeast. And today, on many exposed rocky summits, the glacial signature—scratches in the rock—orient in that direction as well.

During the glacier's maximum advance, about 24,000 years ago, Vermont was beneath more than a mile of ice, more than enough to cover the Green Mountains. As it advanced on its southeasterly course, the ice deepened valleys and smoothed the northwest-facing slopes of

Green Mountain peaks. As it continued past the summit of a given peak, however, the glacier could pluck and carry away huge chunks of rock from the south-facing slope. As a result, some of our mountains tend to have gentler slopes on their north side and steeper slopes, even cliff faces, on their south side. Camel's Hump is perhaps the most obvious example. Long Trail hikers take note: blame those glaciers for making your knees throb and ache on those steep southbound descents.

As the climate warmed and glaciers retreated northward, they left behind lakes, rivers, and, importantly, all the stuff the ice had collected and carried—chunks of mountain, boulders, gravel, sand, silt, and clays strewn and deposited in various patterns across the landscape. By about 13,500 years ago, the glacier had retreated to roughly the Canadian border. Behind the receding ice, the landscape was prepped like a clean canvas for what was to come—colonization by plants, animals, even a little mushroom, and, eventually, a 265-mile-long trail running through it all.

Wild blueberries alongside the trail.

A TRAIL OF COMMUNITIES

Enough history. Let us get out on today's trail, into the green, to find the bird with the odd sex life. To discover the Bicknell's thrush, to learn your daily lesson in humility, and to understand and fully appreciate the nature of the Long Trail, you must climb a mountain. Take Mount Grant, for example, or actually most any high mountain on the Long Trail.

Any given climb is, at its most basic, a walk in the woods. Surrounding you might be a dozen tree species, scores of herbaceous plants, a kingdom of animals, from black bear to black fly to bacteria, a medley of lichens, liverworts, mosses, and (of course) mushrooms. The variety can make a hiker's natural compass spin. But fear not this diversity. Just point yourself uphill. There is a pattern to these woods, a harmony to your walk—the harmony of "natural communities."

Opposite: This lacy waterfall is above Smugglers' Notch, near the Long Trail north of Taft Lodge.

We used to call it habitat, the place where things live outside (and where Long Trail hikers walk). But the natural community model is broader and better than the term *habitat*, and it is a fine way for hikers to gain a sense of where they are on the trail and what is around them. Here is one of many definitions of natural community: a distinct assemblage of living things that interact with one another and their environment. So rather than just a bog, the bog natural community

Cruising through a northern hardwood forest on the slopes of the Green Mountains.

encompasses the particular birds, butterflies, bacteria, and everything else that conspire specifically to be life in a bog. Rather than a stand of evergreen woods, the natural community includes the mammals, mosses, mushrooms, and other organisms that collaborate to be the soul of those evergreen woods. Climate is also a player in the identity of natural communities. Vermont lies in the path of some particularly wild weather, even wilder in the mountains. So where the soil and bedrock and climate are just right for it, a given natural community can reoccur across the landscape.

Vermont has about eighty defined natural communities, each a more or less distinct association of organisms. The Long Trail passes through at least a dozen of them; yet much of the time it traverses only a few, and they are fairly easy to recognize.

Above: Red trillium.
Below: Hobblebush.

CLIMBING THROUGH NATURAL COMMUNITIES

A Long Trail climb often begins in a northern hardwood natural community. Broad-leafed trees dominate: sugar maple, yellow birch, and American beech, with occasional red maple, white ash, and black cherry. Eastern hemlock and red spruce are among occasional evergreens here. But the hardwoods are the signature forests of Vermont, offering us maple syrup, firewood, furniture, blazing fall foliage, and home for everything from warblers to white-tailed deer.

Shrubs and herbaceous plants in these woods are among Vermont's most familiar greenery. One is hobblebush, a spreading shrub that can indeed impede a bushwhacker's progress. This plant, with oval leaves about the size of your palm, might not get a hiker's attention. But take a closer look at hobblebush, for it plays a brilliant game of deception each spring. Its white flowers, displayed in clusters along a branch, are rather puny and inelegant. So hobblebush surrounds each cluster with a ring of larger, showier paper-white blooms. These flowers are infertile imposters. They cannot produce fruits but look good enough to attract insect pollinators toward the real flowers, which go on to generate clusters of apple-red fruits, which, unfortunately, aren't edible unless you're a bird or some critter other than *Homo sapiens.* Yet stick with hobblebush through fall. Its leaves progress like fireworks through stages of purple, rust, and brown, often keeping a few veins of green for good measure. Hobblebush is a Long Trail hiker's personal fall foliage, invisible to leaf peepers who never get far from the car.

Closer yet to the ground in northern hardwoods is a carpet of fern, moss, and other herbaceous plants, some of which are among our most artful and elegant spring wildflowers: the nodding yellow blooms of trout lily, the luscious red trillium, the odd Jack-in-the-pulpit and late-summer-flowering whorled wood aster. Intermediate wood fern and shining clubmoss, among many other ankle-high plants, are constant companions in northern hardwoods. The shrub and herbaceous layer beneath all those broad-leafed trees can lend these woods a lush, junglelike atmosphere.

Above: Trout lilies, an early spring ephemeral familiar to all hikers. Below: Fall foliage, birches.

Opposite: Spring wildflowers decorate the slopes of this mountainside forest near Bennington.

No hiker on the Long Trail is ever far from northern hardwoods. And anyone in these woods will generally be below 2,700 feet in elevation. Not high enough to reach Bicknell's thrush, however. So climb farther upward through the hardwoods toward another natural community. Along the way, the maple and beech and other hardwood species will gradually yield to evergreen trees more tolerant of the poor soils and harsher climate of higher elevations. This is the second dominant woods of the Long Trail, the natural community known as the montane spruce–fir forest.

The montane spruce–fir forest feels like the north. It gives a hiker a sense of elevation and higher latitude. These are the trademark woods of many of the Long Trail's three-thousand-footers. It is cloudier and colder up here. The evergreens, mostly balsam fir and red spruce, like it that way. Lichens dangle from their branches and spread across their trunks. A few hardwood species can thrive among these evergreens— a higher-elevation maple, aptly called mountain maple, for example, and mountain ash, which really isn't an ash but whose dangling red fruits help nourish songbirds on the trail.

A dense evergreen canopy and more acidic soils limit the herbaceous ground cover to bluebead lily, with its elegant yellow flower and grape-blue fruits; bunchberry, a tiny dogwood producing a white bouquet of flowers and a bunch of red fruits; Canada mayflower, a small lily perhaps best recognized by a lone, upright leaf; and an assembly of other hearty plants. Mosses and ground-dwelling lichens form an inviting carpet at a hiker's feet. The mud and puddles aren't as inviting. Yet they are more common in this natural community because soils tend to be shallower and closer to bedrock, which means water has fewer places to travel (apart from inside a hiker's boot). It also means that soil erosion and exposed roots (slippery when wet) are more common on the trail in these woods.

A black bear cub makes a rare appearance. Though bears are widespread throughout the Green Mountains, they are wary of humans and seldom seen.

FELLOW CREATURES OF THE LONG TRAIL

Alert readers may have noticed that animals appear to have been slighted in this discussion of the nature of the Long Trail. It is a valid criticism. The scientists who define natural communities also tend to be botanists. So a bias toward plants is revealed in these definitions and descriptions. It is somewhat understandable, however, because plants, unable to move (except when their seeds do it for them), are more or less a fixture in their respective natural communities. Many animals are not. To be sure, northern hardwoods or montane spruce–fir forests each host a particular assemblage of animals. Bicknell's thrush, for example, is a classic montane specialist; it will not nest down low in the hardwoods. But plenty of Long Trail animals tend to be generalists that thrive in various community types. So rather than getting particular with animals in each natural community, and before we discover the lofty thrush, here is a condensed hiker's guide to wildlife, beginning with the Long Trail's mightiest beast:

The Black Fly — We can stipulate that not everything about the nature of the Long Trail is wonderful. Peak season for this miniature biting machine runs to about July (sometimes later). Females lay their eggs in running water, where the wiggling larvae, anchored to a rock, feed by filtering water rushing by until they transform themselves into flying adults. Once airborne as an adult black fly, only the female will bite. She needs blood from hikers and other animals to nourish eggs that will become yet another generation of black flies to bite yet another round of hikers. When the black fly season ends, however, the mosquitoes take over with slightly less vengeance. Larger biting members of a group of many species known collectively as deer flies will intermittently annoy a hiker who isn't packing an eight-pound sledgehammer in order to slow them down with a swift and direct wallop.

An early hairstreak, one of many butterflies found in Vermont.

Butterflies — These gossamer insects are solar powered, so they are not that common in the shaded woods. Indeed, the shocking blue-green and orange early hairstreak flies high in the canopy of stands of American beech (on whose leaves it lays eggs), dropping into a hiker's world only now and then. Even so, roughly fifty species of butterfly may flap somewhere along or near the Long Trail at various periods from spring through fall. Among the most obvious, in spring, is the Canadian tiger swallowtail, large and yellow with bold black stripes. Flying throughout the hiking season on sunny summits is Milbert's tortoiseshell, whose wings have a flaming red-orange border and a row of tiny iridescent blue jewels. This light show vanishes, however, when Milbert's tortoiseshell snaps its wings closed over its body to conceal itself from predators in the guise of a dead leaf.

A red eft contemplates the day.

Amphibians and Reptiles — Speaking of dead leaves, if one of them hops at your foot, it is most likely an American toad, perhaps the most frequently encountered amphibian on the Long Trail. The alert hiker will know a toad simply by the sound of its hop, noticeably sluggish by comparison to birds and small mammals that jump or scoot trailside with a bit more verve. Far more obvious, in day-glow orange, which is wildlife parlance for "eat me if you dare," is the red eft, actually the teenaged form (and terrestrial, for up to eight years) of the greenish salamander called the eastern newt, which moves to ponds for the rest of its adult life. Yet one of the most abundant Long Trail slimy things (apart from slugs on a wet day) is rarely ever seen — the eastern

Porcupine numbers have been reduced by fishers in recent years.

Deer mice often find Long Trail shelters inviting.

red-backed salamander. Untold numbers of these sit quietly in the leaf litter of mature hardwoods and mixed forests. Step a few feet off trail and flip fallen logs to find this elegant, slender salamander with, as it turns out, a red back. One of the Long Trail's few shortcomings is that it lacks lizards. The garter snake is the trail's most common reptile species; hikers here need not worry about poisonous snakes.

Fisher — This weasel is a yard of terror, even if half its length is bushy brown tail. Fishers hunt mostly at night, which means hikers do not get to see them. In my own travels on the Long Trail and its side trails, more than one thousand miles in total, I have encountered but one fisher, which crossed my path on Whiteface Mountain a mere five feet in front of me, its head down all the while as it passed. More or less elusive on the trail are other members of the weasel family—ermine, mink, long-tailed weasel, and river otter. Agile (and deadly) on land and in trees, a fisher will eat snowshoe hare, squirrels, rodents, fruit, mast (primarily beechnuts), birds, frogs, and most anything else unfortunate enough to cross its zigzag path through the woods. Yet most noteworthy on the fisher's plate is next on our wildlife checklist.

Porcupine — How does one eat a porcupine? Carefully, goes the well-worn reply. Yet fishers don't do cliché. With speed and agility they dart repeatedly to bite the face of a porcupine, ultimately dining, in the absence of quills, from the belly inward. So relentless is the fisher as a predator, that porcupine numbers over the past few decades have plunged in step with Vermont's rising fisher population. This population decline has left the trail lacking one of its primary legends. Hikers no longer worry about porcupines gnawing away at trail shelters each night or even stealing boots for a salty meal of shoe leather.

Rodents — A pejorative name for a group of animals, to be sure, particularly if mice have raided your food bag. (The porcupine is also a rodent.) But let us not forget that this group includes some of the Long Trail's most constant hiking companions — red squirrel, which prefers softwoods and mixed woods, and gray squirrel and eastern chipmunk, both of which are fond of hardwoods.

Cats and Dogs — Apart from tracks or scat on the trail, hikers rarely encounter the wild ones: bobcat, eastern coyote, red fox, and gray fox. To the best of our knowledge, wolves aren't walking the Long Trail's woods (at least not yet).

You may or may not see these creatures on your hike, but rest assured, they are not far away. Clockwise, from top left: Milbert's tortoiseshell (butterfly), ruffed grouse, bobcat, and red squirrel. The tall beech tree shows scars left by a visiting bear.

Moose numbers have climbed in Vermont as the forest cover has returned to high elevations.

The loud, insistent call of the ovenbird is heard well into summer in the forest.

Black Bear — Unless a hiker carelessly sets a table for them, bears want little to do with anyone on the trail. Bears tend to be more common in hardwood forests, where their wide-ranging diet includes beechnuts. Most any hiker who has logged some miles on the Long Trail has probably walked past a bear either hiding somewhere nearby or perhaps even up above in an American beech gorging on its fruits. Claw marks on large beeches all along the trail offer evidence. In any event, the bear can smell even the cleanest hiker long before he or she has a clue of its presence. It is said on the Long Trail that when a fir needle drops to the forest floor, the hawk sees it, the deer hears it, and the bear smells it. As we shall soon discover, our little mushroom, *Marasmius androsaceus,* takes note as well.

Moose — Encountering the largest animal in the woods is an aspiration of most any self-respecting hiker. It is now more likely on the Long Trail as moose numbers have climbed in Vermont during the past few decades. The trail's northern sections host the highest moose densities. During hiking season, moose tend to escape the heat and biting insects in ponds and wetlands; so approach those quietly. In fall and winter, moose move toward higher ground. Hikers should keep a safe, respectful distance from all wildlife, particularly moose during the fall rutting season.

Birds — Little else in nature offers a hiker the blend of flight, song, color, and grace found only in the lives of birds. Binoculars aren't always necessary; a slow and stealthy hiker can hike with many of the Long Trail's bird species. The spring hiking season begins during the peak of breeding season, when some of our most colorful species — vireos, kinglets, thrushes, warblers, tanagers — are singing and raising young. The bird that explodes from the understory (and invariably startles a hiker) is the ruffed grouse, also known in Vermont as partridge. The trail in a few locations passes by nesting peregrine falcons. And fall hikers often walk with southbound migrants, many of which prefer to move in the mountains, including hawks that float high on rising thermals of warm air so that they can glide southbound for miles and miles with nary a flap of wing.

HIGHER STILL

A fine location from which to watch those hawks is the open air of krummholz, which is a German word for "crooked wood." It is also the next step skyward in our progression of natural communities. Krummholz is a forest of trees at their highest altitude on the Long Trail, usually above 3,500 feet. All that remains still higher is bedrock and Vermont's highest plants. Up here wind, ice, snow, rain, and depleted soils conspire to stress the trees so that they grow stunted and twisted. The krummholz is a short, impenetrable version of montane spruce–fir forests with some high-elevation alpine plants making their first appearance. It is some of the Long Trail's most unforgiving turf. It is also where a hiker might discover Bicknell's thrush.

A Bicknell's thrush on its nest with nestlings. These rare thrushes line their nest with horsehair fungus, a tiny forest mushroom.

This famous Vermont songbird breeds near the summits of the Long Trail's highest peaks. The Bicknell's thrush winters on islands in the Caribbean and migrates to the mountains of the Northeast and nearby Atlantic Canada to feast on insects and raise young. This little brown bird actually prefers the upper end of the montane spruce–fir forest. But a hiker standing taller than the treetops in krummholz can sometimes look down toward the montane spruce–fir to find male Bicknell's thrushes launching skyward to sing for a mate like an ethereal flute. It is a serious turn-on for female thrushes (or even Long Trail hikers out for a few cheap thrills).

George J. Wallace, GMC lodge caretaker from 1933 to 1935, is shown with an immature Bicknell's thrush he studied while on the mountain. Wallace later became a professional ornithologist.

Incidentally, up here in thrushland, *Marasmius androsaceus*, our little mushroom, sporting its ebony stalk and tiny cap, is sprouting everywhere. Dig one up and you will find that it can be somewhat discriminating in its choice of sites from which to grow skyward. The mushroom will often sprout directly from a solitary fallen fir needle, sometimes at a perfect right angle to the needle from its tip.

But back to the birds for a moment. A singing bird is most often a male that has established a territory on which to breed; he sings to broadcast his presence and show his turf to females and to defend it all from other intruding males. But Bicknell's thrushes don't work that way. To be sure, the males sing. But it is the female who sets up and maintains the territory, leaving the landless males to fly to and fro across the mountain summit in a frenzied attempt to copulate with multiple females. It is a rare and odd breeding behavior.

Bicknell's thrushes build their nests in the dense protection of spruce and fir, which makes them very hard to find. But should you happen upon one, the nest will most likely be lined with black strands that resemble moose hair or wiry fern roots. Many songbirds nesting on Long Trail mountains use this material in the construction of their nests. Biologists studying Bicknell's thrush in the 1930s noticed the strands but never figured out exactly what they were. Only recently have they solved the mystery.

Those strands are neither fur nor hair nor roots at all. As it happens, one of our rarest songbirds chooses to line its nest with filaments from a rather obscure organism—a little mushroom known as *Marasmius androsaceus*, which sometimes goes by the name horsehair fungus. Invisible as it is to most hikers, our mushroom turns out to be critical in the life of one of the Long Trail's most threatened bird species. Why? Perhaps the strands, threadlike components called rhizomorphs, may have antibacterial properties. Or maybe they're just comfortable to a bird's behind. We're not entirely sure. Whatever the reason, the prosaic *Marasmius androsaceus* and the poetic Bicknell's thrush are two players among the many performing in the theater of nature on the Long Trail.

When a Bicknell's thrush lands on a fir bough near the summit of Mount Grant, an alert hiker may now envision a chain of events. A fir needle breaks loose and drops to the forest floor. From that single needle the following spring may sprout a tiny mushroom, later to be carried by a little brown bird to a nest that will host—for this trail and for its visitors—yet another generation of Bicknell's thrushes.

Every event along this trail can be remarkable; every event can matter: the song of a thrush, the spore of a mushroom, the step of a hiker, even the falling to earth of a single fir needle. So from that halfway spot on Mount Grant, walk either north or south on the Long Trail. It doesn't really matter. Your trip is more than a hike. This trail is your long, green journey into one of the greatest natural dramas on earth.

Opposite: A timberline sign on Camel's Hump warns hikers to tread softly, whatever the season.

FURTHER READING

Readers who seek more wisdom on the rock beneath Vermont (and the life above it) may consult *The Nature of Vermont*, a classic by Charles W. Johnson.

The seminal work on Vermont's natural communities, which informs and inspires this account, is *Wetland, Woodland, Wildland: A Guide to the Natural Communities of Vermont* by Elizabeth H. Thompson and Eric R. Sorenson.

A handy and attractive guide to natural communities, plants, animals, geology, and more along the trail is *GMC Nature Guide to Vermont's Long Trail* (2008) by Lexi Shear.

CLIMBING TO THE ARCTIC IN VERMONT

BY CHARLES W. JOHNSON

Perched atop a few of Vermont's highest peaks sit small areas of low-lying vegetation, a landscape in miniature, similar in many ways to the vast treeless tundra of the Arctic a thousand miles to the north. These are natural plant communities ecologists call *alpine meadows*, a term that captures both their geography and outward appearance. *Arctic-alpine tundra* is an older designation, evoking the mysterious, grand landscape beyond tree line in Canada.

Such natural communities are rare in Vermont, occurring only in small swaths on three mountain summits, all above 4,000 feet: 250 acres on Mount Mansfield, 10 on Camel's Hump, and less than half an acre on Mount Abraham. To see larger expanses, you have to travel to the high peaks of central Maine and Mount Katahdin, the Adirondacks of New York, or the White Mountains in New Hampshire—or, of course, to northern Canada.

Wherever alpine meadows exist, environmental conditions live up to the characterization "Arctic"—a tough place indeed for any living thing. Going up is going north: a thousand-foot rise in elevation equates to roughly five hundred miles of northward latitude and a temperature drop of more than 3 degrees Fahrenheit. The mean annual temperature at the top of Mount Mansfield, for example, is just above freezing (33 degrees), while four thousand feet lower in Burlington, near Lake Champlain, it is 45 degrees.

The waxy blooms of diapensia brighten the alpine zone each spring.

Vermont's record high is 105 degrees, but for Mount Mansfield it is only 85. Winter is long in the alpine meadows and the frost-free growing season short, usually less than ninety days, sometimes much less. Wind, a regular presence all year and here unimpeded by trees or topography, is physically and physiologically punishing. In summer, exposure to wind and sun dries out soils and plants quickly. At other times, wind-borne snow and ice crystals batter and shear plants into contorted shapes. The soil is essentially peat—organic plant matter that, in the brief, cool summers, does not have the time to decompose completely. It is nutrient-poor, acidic, thin, sparse, sensitive to trampling, and, on steeper sections, at risk of erosion.

Yet Vermont alpine meadows differ in significant ways from true Arctic tundra; there are marked variations in plant species and composition between the two areas. First is sheer size: Vermont's are tiny—a few acres compared to Canada's half a million square miles of tundra—a simple physical limitation to biological abundance and diversity. They experience a year-round daily day/night cycle (highly varied by season), while the Arctic has prolonged periods of twenty-four-hour dark (winter) and twenty-four-hour light (summer). While a great deal of the Arctic is "polar desert," receiving little precipitation throughout the year, the tundra is often water-saturated and boggy since it is underlain by permafrost (permanently frozen ground), which in summer is kept from thawing by the topmost layers of insulating peat and therefore acts as a barrier to downward water percolation. Vermont's alpine meadows, on the other hand, receive a great deal of precipitation (an average annual amount from clouds, rain, and snow of seventy-five inches, more than twice that in the Champlain Valley), but high winds, sun, steep terrain, and lack of permafrost may quickly turn them bone-dry, "polar deserts" of their own. An ecological irony!

So how do plants cope in such an exacting place? They must be specially adapted simply to survive—"flourish" is hardly

ever an apt term! Lichens of several crusty species spread themselves flat over the barest, most exposed rocks. In more protected places, where soil has accumulated, other plants manage to grow. Most are dwarfed, with tough, often thick leaves, characteristics caused both by severity of climate and lack of soil nutrients. (The same plants in milder, enriched locales grow larger and more robustly and have softer leaves.) Many also grow in compact, low-lying mats tucked into crevices and recesses in the rocks. Thus, plants can keep a low profile to desiccating winds and abrading ice, while retaining what warmth there is.

Flowering plants also get on with business quickly in the compressed, ephemeral spring. They bloom early, some even when snow is still present, in a delicate yet stunning display near the ground. By fall, virtually all species produce overwintering flower buds that blossom the next spring as soon as conditions allow. Most species are perennial and many semievergreen ("wintergreen"), continuing photosynthesis and growth into fall and resuming early in spring. Further, when leaves die they remain attached to the plants within the mats and provide additional protection—a quasi insulation—against the elements. And most of a plant's mass—as much as

Though Vermont's alpine meadows receive much precipitation from rain, snow, and mist, they are always fragile. This alpine bog is on Mount Mansfield.

95 percent in some cases—is in roots and rhizomes (underground stems) hidden within the soil, allowing the plants to store precious food reserves and hold the scant soil in place.

In Vermont, three dozen species or so of Arctic-type plants grow in alpine meadows. Visually dominant are the heaths (mostly shrubs, in the family Ericaceae), such as alpine bilberry (*Vaccinium uliginosum*) and mountain cranberry (*Vaccinium vitis-idaea*), and the sedges (family Cyperaceae), particularly Bigelow's sedge (*Carex bigelowii*). Other typical species are three-toothed cinquefoil (*Potentilla tridentata*), mountain sandwort (*Arenaria groenlandica*), and highland rush (*Juncus trifidus*). Rarer are such species as diapensia (*Diapensia lapponica*), black crowberry (*Empetrum nigrum*), and bearberry willow (*Salix uva-ursi*). Even two trees, balsam fir (*Abies balsamea*) and black spruce (*Picea mariana*), inches tall and hardly recognizable as trees, manage to live hunkered down between the rocks.

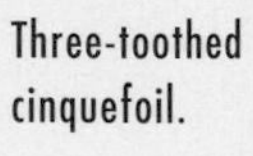

Three-toothed cinquefoil.

For animals, conditions are harsh, food meager, and habitats scant. Aside from the occasional stray moose or bear, a few small mammals (boreal red-backed vole, short-tailed shrew) may be present in ice-free times, but move down to more protected areas for winter. Migratory birds such as dark-eyed juncos and white-throated sparrows may nest here. The rarest of alpine birds, and among the most secretive, the Bicknell's thrush may venture into the meadows from its more secure nesting sites within the adjacent stunted balsam fir and red spruce. Insects, though, both flying and crawling types, are abundant in summer. As with plants, they are a hardy lot, yet many have a delicate beauty that defies locale, such as Milbert's tortoiseshell, a butterfly. Only one species, Arctic ground beetle (*Nebria suturalis*), lives here and nowhere else.

Beyond their ecological significance, these areas are visually stunning in all seasons: carpets of green and blue-green against the green-gray rocks, suddenly lit up with spring blossoms of white, pink, blue, and yellow. In the fall, they become a landscape painted vivid red and purple by heaths and muted tawny yellow by grasses and sedges. Winter brings the ethereal and overwhelming starkness of ice and snow.

Vermont's alpine meadows are likely "relict" natural communities, 10,000-year-old vestiges of the last ice age when the landscape of this region was indeed Arctic. As the mile-thick glacier receded under a warming climate, the tundra communities yielded to the oncoming boreal, then temperate, vegetation and withdrew to ever higher ground. The climate continued to moderate, and from about 8,000 to 5,000 years ago, it was even warmer than today's. The Vermont Arctic took its final refuge on the mountain peaks, where it has persisted so precariously to this day.

The summit ridge of Mount Mansfield, a beautiful and demanding environment.

Despite the venerable history of alpine meadows here, and despite their tenacity in the face of demanding climatic conditions, these are among our most endangered natural areas. Increasing numbers of visitors (walkers, hikers, and their canine companions), especially in the years before protective efforts began, had the biggest, if unintentional, negative impacts on them. Heavy foot traffic into the meadows wore away big patches of vegetation, and by the end of the 1960s, these ecosystems were in jeopardy.

Alarmed by what was happening, the Vermont Department of Forests, Parks and Recreation, the Green Mountain Club, and the University of Vermont jointly took steps. (Mount Mansfield's summit is owned by the University of Vermont, Camel's Hump by the Vermont Department of Forests, Parks, and Recreation, and Mount Abraham by the U.S. Forest Service.) First on Camel's Hump in 1969, then on Mount Mansfield the following year, uniformed summit caretakers began patrolling the summits every day, spring through fall, educating visitors about the areas and the importance of keeping on the trails and off the inviting but fragile "lawns" of rare plants. Now, over forty years later and with over forty thousand visitors to Mount Mansfield alone, the program continues and has succeeded not only in stemming the loss, but actually restoring some previously damaged sections. (The very small meadow on Mount Abraham is severely, perhaps mortally, degraded.)

But another threat, more insidious and less controllable, looms. Global climate change has implications for not just damage to, but outright elimination of, these sensitive ecosystems, along with many others elsewhere in the world. Like beacons over 4,000 feet high in our skies, they are signals that can warn us of dangers ahead and urge us to act before it's too late.

CHAPTER 8

TO MAKE IT LAST FOREVER

Protecting the Long Trail and the Green Mountains

BY SUSAN SHEA

IMAGINE NEARING THE END of a grueling 265-mile trek on the Long Trail and encountering a "No Trespassing, Private Land" sign blocking the trail. Do you turn around and give up your dream of hiking the whole trail? Or continue and risk meeting an irate landowner—even getting arrested? Suppose you decide to continue along the trail. Shortly you hear the sound of hammering and machinery and emerge from the woods into a freshly bulldozed clearing. A new house is going up next to the trail. A piece of Vermont's footpath in the wilderness is compromised, ruined for you and all the hikers to follow.

Fortunately, such scenarios are rare on the Long Trail. But they would have occurred frequently if the Green Mountain Club (GMC) had not undertaken its Long Trail Protection Campaign.

The cliffs of Sugarloaf Mountain catch the spring sunlight high above Hazen's Notch, site of several parcels of protected land.

In 1986, when the club started this program, almost seventy miles of the Long Trail and twenty-two miles of side trails in northern Vermont were located on private land. Since that time, the GMC has made eighty-two separate acquisitions, piecing together a protected corridor along the trail, much as one stitches together a giant patchwork quilt.

This green swath stretches from the Green Mountain National Forest on Mount Ellen in Fayston to the Canadian border and connects Camel's Hump, Mount Mansfield, Hazen's Notch, and Jay State Forests. This strip of conserved land along the spine of the Green Mountains includes the new Long

MILESTONES— AS OF 2009

- Long Trail miles protected: 60
- Long Trail future relocation miles protected: 6.7
- Long Trail miles unprotected: 7.7
- Side trail miles protected: 18
- Side trail miles unprotected: 4.5
- Projects completed: 82
- Acres conserved by GMC: 24,632
- Acres GMC assisted other groups in conserving: 8,929

Trail State Forest, a product of the GMC's twenty-four-year effort. Remarkably, the club has accomplished all this through voluntary agreements with landowners.

Voluntary agreements are not new to the work of the GMC, of course. From the time the trail was originally constructed until the 1980s, it crossed private land through informal handshake agreements with landowners.

But times change, and during the 1980s, several major threats to the trail's integrity arose. In the Winooski River Valley, a house was built on the trail in Jonesville and a radio tower was installed on nearby Robbins Mountain. Both landowners asked the club to move the Long Trail. Other landowners in the vicinity would not allow the trail to cross their land, so it was relocated to the road, subjecting hikers to a four-mile road walk.

In 1985, the club learned that Wagner Woodlands, a timber company, was interested in selling 40,000 acres of its Vermont holdings, including thirteen miles of the Long Trail in the northern towns of Westfield, Montgomery, Lowell, and Eden. This news ignited a discussion among the GMC's board of directors over how best to protect the trail. The club was unsure if new owners would continue to host the trail or if the land would be developed or clear-cut.

As then president Preston Bristow reflected years later, "We couldn't stand by and watch the northern Long Trail be nickeled and dimed to death. It was presumptuous, it was risky, it was like nothing we'd ever done before, but the club had to act. Let the chips fall where they may, we had to shoulder our packs and start down that trail."

In January 1986, the GMC's board appointed a task force to review the status of the trail on privately owned lands and to recommend a strategy "for permanently protecting the continuity and scenic values of the Long Trail." The club's focus was on northern Vermont, because in southern and central sections the trail was located on public lands—the Green Mountain National Forest, state lands, and the Appalachian Trail corridor.

At the May 1986 annual meeting, GMC president Bristow reported that the Vermont General Assembly had passed legislation, introduced by then representative Howard Dean, that offered to match funds the club raised for trail protection.

Opposite: Looking north from Belvidere Mountain toward Jay Peak and Big Jay, the forests of the Meltzer Tract include three miles of the Long Trail and several miles of side trails. The tract was acquired by the Green Mountain Club in 1987.

Ted Vogt flagging a boundary.

ADVENTURES OF A CORRIDOR MONITOR

BY TED VOGT

Ted Vogt, who wanders the woods for the Green Mountain Club's Stewardship Program, recounts some of his experiences.

Late in the day on my first visit to the remote northern Vermont property I had been assigned as a volunteer GMC corridor monitor, I was crawling on my belly through an extended thicket of "dog-hair" spruce, seriously doubting my backcountry skills.

I had hoped to find one more faded blaze along the boundary before calling it quits, but the spruce threw me off. There were no blazes on the other side. When I tried to circumvent the spruce on my return, I realized I had completely lost my line. The marshy area off to my right looked familiar—until I reached an identical marshy area a little farther on. It occurred to me that getting lost the first time out was not going to enhance my reputation back at the club.

Happily I found my way out before dark by following a tiny spring that flowed into a brook that eventually crossed the logging road I had walked in on.

These lands the club has protected are jewels—they are Vermont's past and its future. Walking these extraordinary properties is a privilege and an adventure. A favorite spot of mine is a narrow ravine, high on the northeast flank of Tillotson Peak. There, a small brook cascades steeply down the mountain over boulders to a marshy shelf far below. Several large yellow birch and beech trees grow improbably out of the walls of the ravine. Views east are spectacular. This small place—only one hundred yards off the Long Trail, but invisible from it—seems utterly wild.

Ferns line the Long Trail in many lowland sections.

In 2001, then governor Howard Dean completed his end-to-end hike of the Long Trail at the Canadian border. Dean was instrumental in getting the Vermont Legislature to appropriate money for land acquisition to protect the trail.

RISING TO THE CHALLENGE

The club had never mounted a capital campaign before and had no experience in land conservation, but with serious threats to the trail escalating rapidly and no one else responsible for its protection, something had to be done—and quickly. On May 24, 1986, the GMC's board established the Long Trail Protection Fund, and soon afterwards an experienced fund-raiser, Bob Lincoln, was hired.

Early in the campaign, two substantial gifts were made. One was from Aldie Gannett, wife of Senator Robert T. Gannett. Kimball Simpson, now chair of the GMC's Land Protection Committee, recalls, "Aldie was a driving force behind the campaign. She would show up at meetings of the fund-raising committee with a can of chocolate chip cookies in one hand and a check in the other."

In the late 1980s, Senator Patrick Leahy secured an $150,000 appropriation for the National Park Service, which funded research into landownership along the northern Long Trail and the first set of maps showing property boundaries. In 1990, the Vermont Legislature, with the support of then lieutenant governor Dean and Senators Robert Gannett and Dick Mazza, began making regular appropriations for the GMC to acquire Long Trail lands. Since then, the legislature has contributed $4.5 million, which has been critical to the success of the program. The Vermont Housing and Conservation Board has awarded several major grants for specific land acquisitions and helped fund the club's land protection and stewardship staff. And the GMC has raised over $5 million in private funds. "It's been an extraordinary example of a highly successful public-private partnership," says Simpson.

More than 33,000 acres of important lands on or near the Long Trail System have been protected over the years by the GMC and allied organizations.

Important GMC fund-raising initiatives have included the 265-Mile Club for donors contributing $1,000 or more and a hike-a-thon. Board member Bob Northrop raised more than $215,000 with two end-to-end hikes celebrating his seventy-fifth and eightieth birthdays. Two granddaughters of one of the Three Musketeers (the first women to complete the trail) hiked end-to-end to raise money for trail protection. They called themselves "The Musketeers Two." Dan Houston, a member from Ohio who suffers from Parkinson's disease, raised funds for both the Long Trail and Parkinson's research on his hike. Comments Lincoln, "We have received donations from all over the country. The number of people who love the trail and the Green Mountains is impressive. The club's membership and volunteers have played an enormous role in our success. Their willingness to stay the course has been the key."

PUTTING THE PIECES TOGETHER

While most landowners have cooperated by allowing the trail to cross their land, Kimball Simpson tells the story of one property owner who was visited by club staff in the early stages of the program to discuss a possible land purchase: "'There's something I want to show you before we start talking,' said the owner. He took Harry Peet down to his basement where there was a whole stack of freshly painted signs that said 'Long Trail Closed.' That's what we were up against."

The Vermont Chapter of The Nature Conservancy provided invaluable assistance early on, when much land crossed by the Long Trail was on the market. The first parcel, the 171-acre Riendeau Tract in Jay, was acquired in 1987. The same year the 1,946-acre Meltzer Tract in Lowell, which includes three miles of the Long Trail, two side trails, Tillotson Camp, and the summit of Belvidere Mountain, was purchased. In 1990, the club hired its own staff to negotiate land

Near Belvidere Mountain, the Long Trail passes by Lockwood Pond, host to beavers and other wildlife. The pond is located on the GMC's Meltzer Tract and is therefore protected.

In 1991, the GMC acquired the land surrounding Journey's End Camp and the Journey's End Trail, an important piece of property at the northern terminus of the Long Trail. The old Journey's End Camp, shown above, has been moved to the GMC headquarters in Waterbury Center and a new shelter has been erected in the vicinity.

acquisitions with a grant from the Vermont Housing and Conservation Board. Susan Shea, the GMC's first director of land protection, contacted all Long Trail landowners, even if their land was not on the market, beginning a process of cultivation that paid off in scores of land and easement acquisitions and miles of trail protected.

The club has bid for land at auction, at tax sale, swapped land parcels, rescued land that was to be developed, and even buried a donor's ashes on land he donated. Anything to protect the Long Trail! Some negotiations with landowners have lasted as long as ten years. Looking back, past GMC president Brian Fitzgerald commented, "It's been a really successful program. I've been surprised the club has been able to make so much progress without the federal involvement of National Scenic Trail designation. In a lot of ways it has transformed the GMC from a small, low-key hiking club into more of a conservation organization, a good thing for the club in the long-term."

Above: *Clintonia* (bluebead lily) in blossom.

Right: In several locations on the Long Trail, such as here, south of Johnson, hikers and loggers coexist. As part of the Long Trail Protection Program, the GMC has worked to relocate the Long Trail in places where it follows logging or other roads. Careful timber harvesting is allowed on GMC lands outside a buffer zone protecting the Long Trail.

The GMC's preference is to acquire a minimum of a thousand-foot-wide buffer centered on the trail. In many places the club has purchased additional land to protect side trails, wildlife habitat, rare plant species, or other trails, such as segments of the Catamount Trail (Vermont's long-distance cross-country ski trail). Most of the land the GMC acquires is transferred to state ownership, with the club retaining a trail right-of-way and conservation restrictions on the land to ensure that the trail is permanently protected as a backcountry area.

A cooperative relationship with the staff of the Vermont Department of Forests, Parks, and Recreation for both land acquisition and stewardship has enabled the state and the GMC to achieve more than either entity could have alone. An example of this collaboration was the dedication of the new Long Trail State Forest in 1993; it includes the section of the trail between Route 15 in Johnson and Route 242 in Jay. In areas where private landowners prefer to retain ownership, such as some ski areas, the club has obtained conservation easements or simple trail easements to ensure the right of passage.

In the process of protecting the trail, the GMC's Long Trail Protection Campaign has created a magnificent wildlife corridor stretching the length of the northern Green Mountains, connecting large areas of core wildlife habitat in Vermont and across the border in the Sutton Mountains of Canada. Hikers benefit, of course; and so do moose, black bear, bobcats, fishers, deer, coyotes, hawks, songbirds, and many other creatures.

Ravens are often high-altitude companions of hikers on the Long Trail.

I had a personal encounter with one of those "beneficiaries" some years ago. As I drove around a curve on Route 242 in Jay Pass one rainy summer afternoon, a cow moose stood in the road a hundred feet from my car. It had come off the Atlas Tract on the south side of the highway, which we had recently purchased, and was heading onto the Big Jay Tract, which the club had previously protected.

The moose stared at me, oblivious to ownership and property boundaries. As I met its gaze, I felt good that we had preserved the animal's home.

STEWARDS OF THE LAND

Once the land is conserved, the GMC's responsibilities do not end. To ensure the trail experience is protected over the long term, the club must monitor these conservation lands and resolve or prosecute any easement violations.

"I was at the Long Trail parking area on Route 105 in Jay," recalls volunteer corridor monitor Cat Eich, "when a guy pulled up in a new six-wheel truck and asked me where the snowmobile trail was. He said he had to do some blasting there the next day. I knew that area was conservation land and a snowmobile trail there wasn't legal. When I reached the site, I saw a swath eight to ten feet wide had been cleared through the woods and graded; the natural slope of the land had been altered. It looked like a major log haul road. The Long Trail could not be found. There were lots of hiker footprints indicating people had been getting lost." The GMC later negotiated with the local snowmobile club to reroute their trail, restore the area as much as possible, and pay damages.

As a result of the Long Trail Protection Campaign, the club manages or co-manages more than eighty properties covering more than 25,000 acres. The GMC owns over 3,000 acres and holds ease-

Big Muddy Pond in Eden. The GMC has protected land near the pond and the Babcock Trail, which leads to the pond.

ments on over 1,000 acres of private land and 20,000 acres of state forest. Some of the work—such as the preparation of management plans, GIS mapping, timber stand improvement on properties enrolled in Vermont's current use program, and enforcement of easement violations—is handled by GMC staff and/or state personnel.

"We've had problems with timber trespass and ATVs, for example," former stewardship coordinator Matt Moore notes. "Since most of our conservation easements are on state land, we work closely with the Vermont Department of Forests, Parks, and Recreation on land management. We carefully consider requests from neighboring landowners to use our conserved lands and have allowed activities such as log skidding and landing, designated cross-country ski trails, and some VAST snowmobile trails."

The club established an endowment fund in 1993 to generate income for stewardship, later named the Aldie Gannett Long Trail Stewardship Fund.

In addition, more than thirty-five volunteer corridor monitors visit every property that the GMC owns or holds an easement on to ensure that conservation restrictions are being upheld. The monitors, trained and supervised by stewardship director Pete Antos-Ketcham, agree to walk the boundaries of their assigned property at least once a year. Often the monitors help locate, clear, and repaint the boundaries and put up signs, reducing the likelihood of unintended violations.

Stewardship is a big job, but the GMC is committed to defending the integrity of the lands it has protected in order to conserve the Long Trail experience.

◆

Today the trail is more than 95 percent protected, but some gaps remain. The GMC is committed to securing the last twelve miles of the 445-mile Long Trail System. "Realistically, it may be another generation before the last piece is secured. This is a willing seller program," says GMC executive director Ben Rose. "But GMC has patience and resolve."

Hiker traversing a rocky cleft on the Long Trail south of Burnt Rock Mountain on land protected by the GMC through a conservation easement.

From left are Little Jay, Big Jay, and Jay Peak. The Big Jay Tract, which protects much of this view, was acquired by the GMC in 1993.

SIGNIFICANT ACQUISITIONS

A MEMORIAL IN HAZEN'S NOTCH

Hazen's Notch is a deep cleft in the Green Mountains beneath the dramatic cliffs of Sugarloaf Mountain, which have been home to peregrine falcons. A luxuriant growth of ferns and wildflowers carpets the forest floor below the cliffs.

In 1992, Mark Dimock sold a piece of land in Hazen's Notch to the Green Mountain Club that included a section of the Long Trail. When he was diagnosed with terminal cancer in 1994, Dimock decided to donate his remaining ninety-six acres in Westfield to the GMC for eventual transfer to the Hazen's Notch State Park. In his will, Dimock stipulated that his ashes were to be buried on the property and a monument was to be erected in memory of his mother, Lucy Butler Stotesbury. The ashes were sent to the club after his death that winter. On a beautiful spring day in 1995, club staff members and Dimock's relatives met for a ceremony to bury his ashes in his beloved woodland, beneath a large boulder with a plaque in memory of his mother. The boulder overlooks a small spring on scenic Route 58.

BURNT ROCK MOUNTAIN

From the top of Burnt Rock Mountain, there are spectacular views in all directions. Just south of the summit, a short spur trail leads through the spruce and fir to the highest glacial pothole in New England. Early in the morning, hikers may hear the song of the rare Bicknell's thrush, which nests here.

In 1997, 3.5 miles of the Long Trail in Fayston and Duxbury, including the summit of Burnt Rock Mountain, were conserved in cooperation with the landowners, the trustees of Big Basin Forest. In a complicated transaction, the GMC acquired a parcel of timberland adjacent to Big Basin's holdings and exchanged it for the protection of the key 702 acres. The summit of Mount Ira Allen, Cowles Cove Shelter, and a section of the Monroe Skyline were also protected by this project.

BLACK FALLS, NORTHERN FOREST JEWEL

Quiet, solitude, remoteness—those are the feelings visitors experience on the 3,764-acre Black Falls Tract. This property, which wraps around the base of the Jay Mountains and includes the Black Falls Basin and Stanhope Ridge, is the largest of the Long Trail Protection Campaign. There black bears feed on abundant beechnuts, rare ferns grace the cliffs, and three big brooks tumble down the mountain, providing spawning areas for native brook trout.

After ten years of effort, in 2001 the GMC closed on this project in Westfield, Montgomery, and Richford. Four miles of the Long Trail overlook this significant conservation property, also an important watershed for the Trout River. The primary funders of this $1.2 million project were the Vermont Housing and Conservation Board; Sweet Water Trust; the Open Space Conservancy, an affiliate of the Open Space Institute; and the federal Land and Water Conservation Fund.

JOURNEY'S END UP FOR AUCTION

In 1991, GMC staff received a call from Orleans County forester George Buzzell, who had heard that the private parcel in Jay that contained the Journey's End Trail and Journey's End Camp would be auctioned off in several days.

After some scrambling, GMC representatives were present for the auction in an abandoned building of the Space Research Corporation. The room was ventilated with broken windows and filled with other bidders, the press, and curious onlookers. Other interested parties were planning to strip the land of its timber and subdivide it for hunting camps. Following a preplanned strategy, the GMC was able to bid successfully on this two-hundred-acre woodland, and avert a disaster for the only access to the northern terminus of the Long Trail.

BOLTON MOUNTAIN UPLANDS

The Long Trail here winds along the wooded ridge between Bolton and Stimson Mountains, up a series of stone steps, around huge boulders left by the glaciers, and past hollow snags frequented by raccoons. Peepers call from a small wetland in the sag to the east. The trail emerges onto an open ledge, where a vista stretches off to the west. Lake Champlain glimmers in the distance.

The GMC acquired 1,080 acres on this ridge from the Bolton Valley Holiday Resort in 2003, protecting 2.5 miles of the Long Trail, Buchanan Shelter, and 0.8 mile of the Catamount Trail. The subalpine spruce-fir forest on the southern slope of Bolton Mountain, an ecological community of statewide significance, which is habitat for the rare Bicknell's thrush, was also conserved.

Part of the Chittenden County Uplands Conservation Project, this tract connects the Mount Mansfield State Forest with important wildlife habitat further west. The Vermont Housing and Conservation Board, the state legislature, the Catamount Trail Association, the Fields Pond Foundation, the Barstow Foundation, the Barstow Charitable Trust, and other donors provided essential funding for this acquisition.

A TRAIL VOLUNTEER'S GENEROSITY

Don Hill started volunteering for the club in 1966, repairing and maintaining Tillotson Camp. For many years he carried a major share of the responsibility for maintaining the trail between Route 242 and the Canadian border. Hill also adopted Roundtop Shelter, Jay Camp, the Jay Loop Trail, and the Babcock Extension. He has built four outhouses and is famous for his handsome, hand-routed trail signs.

When the time came to think about the future of his land in Eden, Hill made a bargain sale of his fourteen acres to the GMC, selling it for $13,000 less than the appraised value. The property is surrounded by the Long Trail State Forest and is visible from the Long Trail parking area and scenic Belvidere Pond. Prior to Hill's gift, the club was concerned that this parcel, which has frontage on Route 118, would be developed.

AFTERWORD

THE TRAIL AHEAD

The Next One Hundred Years

BY BEN ROSE

PREDICTING THE FUTURE is a hazardous business. Sharing assumptions about what will happen a hundred years hence affords one the opportunity to demonstrate to future readers one's quaint, old-fashioned cluelessness about the years to come. Worse, correct forecasts of the future are unremarkable to readers in that future, because at best they seem obvious. Wrong predictions, on the other hand, jump off the page.

These granite summit ledges are colorful every fall.

Many of the assumptions we operate under in 2010 will be moot or wrong long before 2110. Global climate change, for example, is much on our minds in 2010. By 2110, it will probably be either much better or much worse than we now imagine.

Likewise, those of us who have lived half or more of our lives in the twentieth century—the "American century"—are not particularly well equipped to foresee how Vermont will fare economically or as a destination for international visitors. The suspicion is that even in a hundred years, Vermont will still be a bit quaint, off the beaten track, and scenic enough to attract guests. For another example of how hard it is to predict what will happen in the future, look backward to the early days of the Long Trail. When the trail was conceived in 1909, James P. Taylor could not have foreseen the changes that would occur during its first century. Back then, trampers could get to their trailhead starting points by train and horse-drawn carriage. The white blazes of the Long Trail often led through the fields of hill farms where fresh eggs and milk could be purchased. There were no airplanes or cell towers or plans for enormous windmills.

Taylor could not have foreseen that a hundred years later Vermont would be heavily reforested, with abundant deer and moose and beavers and bears and with a real hope for the return of wolves and mountain lions; nor that private automobiles would have supplanted public transport as the preferred mode of access to trailheads. Nor that the world's human population would be approaching seven billion. Nor that injured hikers would be able to call for help on handheld wireless communications devices.

AN IRONIC REVERSAL

Although Taylor has been given much credit as an early Long Trail visionary, another role that he fills in the "creation myth" of the Long Trail is as the main character in a tale of irony. In the 1930s, just two short decades after the formation of the Green Mountain Club (GMC), Taylor resurfaced in Vermont history as the founding executive director of the Vermont Chamber of Commerce. In that capacity, he was a vocal proponent for the proposed Green Mountain Parkway, a New Deal public works project proposed for Vermont that would have created jobs and stimulated Vermont's moribund Depression economy by constructing a high-elevation paved scenic road, akin to Virginia's Blue Ridge Parkway. It would have cut the Long Trail to ribbons, and the GMC was strongly opposed.

When the citizens of Vermont voted by a narrow margin to oppose the project, the debate pitted an earlier vision of how the Vermont landscape could be enhanced against one of that vision's earliest and most vocal proponents. Taylor had moved on in his own thinking to promote a more "modern"—and less romantic—landscape aesthetic. This story, as much as any other, encapsulates Vermont's blessedly contrarian response to the twentieth century.

Who could foresee in 1910 that the GMC, which began with 24 members, would have 10,000 members a century later? Who could foresee that 200,000 people per year would hike on the Long Trail, or that the GMC would become a major landowner and easement holder out of necessity to protect the trail corridor and the ridgeline of the Green Mountains from encroaching development? Yet such has been the case.

It is hard to predict what the major pressures will be on the Long Trail in its second century without making broad assumptions about everything that will happen socially, politically, environmentally, and technologically. However, at the risk of future ridicule, I venture these predictions:

- The Long Trail will survive as a continuous footpath between Massachusetts and Quebec, and the GMC will hold a big bicentennial celebration in 2110.
- The Long Trail will become increasingly rare and precious as a relatively quiet and unspoiled pedestrian-only backcountry footpath.
- Demand for the "Long Trail experience" will continue to increase. Trail managers will need to respond to continued growth in overall use. As gasoline is supplemented or replaced by other fuels, modes of transportation will change accordingly. There will be a return to more communal forms of trailhead access.
- Access to at least some of the most popular trailheads will become more concentrated, limited, and/or regulated. Will we be required to charge

A misty day on the Long Trail.

trail fees? We don't know. How will the Long Trail's maintenance and upkeep be paid for? Will public funding remain available? For the record, from the perspective of 2010, we want the trail to remain free and believe that people should not be required to pay a fee each time they set foot on their public land.

- Competing land uses along Vermont's ridgelines will become more intense. Communications, wind energy, water supply, ecosystem services (such as habitat for rare and endangered species), and demand for residential properties will all stake powerful claims to specific portions of the Long Trail corridor.
- The GMC will face ever-increasing pressures as a steward of land and easement interests. The assumption that the trail is "protected" merely by being located on public land (i.e., in state or federal ownership) may not stand up to the pressures of the decades ahead.

For example, in 2007, there was a terrible easement violation on Big Jay Mountain. Two men with chainsaws cut an illegal swath to create a wide-open ski chute down the face of Big Jay, which had been acquired by the GMC in 1993 and deeded to the state of Vermont with an ecologically protective easement. This criminal act created a scar on a "protected" property. The assumption that the Long Trail will survive for a second century hinges on the broad assumption that the rule of law will be in effect as a general social condition. If, contrary to that smug assumption, this easement violation proves to be the tip of an iceberg and anarchy increases in the backcountry, all bets are off. The

GMC executive director Ben Rose and daughter Anya hiked a lengthy section of the Long Trail together in the summer of 2008.

Big Jay easement violation of 2007 demonstrates the increasing pressure on public land for other forms of recreation and the increasing urgency of promoting a Leave No Trace ethic among all outdoor enthusiasts.

In 1910, the mountains of Vermont were in the process of being abandoned, as hill farms disappeared. A long, slow "rewilding" had begun. In 2010, Vermont's mountains once again present themselves to tens of millions of Americans and Canadians as a remote, heavily forested "frontier." How will we treat Vermont's wild high places the second time around?

To what extent will the growing global demand for resources (water, energy, timber) impact on the management priorities for public lands in Vermont? The Long Trail's character as a "footpath in the wilderness" may diminish in direct proportion to growth in Vermont's population.

Our sense of place, and particularly the fragile perception of wildness, can be disrupted by subdivision, residential construction, new roads, and driveways. It doesn't take much to change the character of a piece of trail.

On the other hand, the Long Trail is an extremely robust concept. It links two facts that will remain true in a hundred years: First, the political borders of Vermont are with Canada in the north and Massachusetts in the south and walking from one to the other is a long walk. And second, Vermont ain't flat. It has mountains that are old, weathered, but substantially higher than what most people along the eastern seaboard usually see. They are real mountains, and they will outlast us. The romantic appeal of walking Vermont's ridgeline will last as long as the mountains.

Because the Long Trail is a Vermont phenomenon, Vermonters will continue to cherish it and protect it as part of their heritage. We are fiercely loyal to this trail. That loyalty will continue and may prove to be even more resilient than some of our other twentieth-century icons, such as maple syrup, dairy farms, colorful fall foliage, and old barns.

Organizationally, the greatest challenges for the GMC as maintainer and protector of the Long Trail will be

- achieving financial sustainability through the accumulation and preservation of capital (i.e., building an endowment sufficient to distribute a significant percentage of annual operating fund) and
- continuing to attract, develop, and rely upon volunteer leadership despite all the other pressures and opportunities that compete for people's time. The story of the GMC's second century, like the story of its first, will be a story of the individual leaders, trail workers, and assorted volunteers who "step up" to invest energy and vision in the Long Trail's future.

◆

The Long Trail is a precious Vermont legacy. Pass it on! Happy one hundredth birthday, GMC!

This view south from Baker Peak is evidence that "the romantic appeal of walking Vermont's ridgeline will last as long as the mountains."

Following spread: The view west from the summit of Camel's Hump in fall is a reward to last a lifetime.

INDEX

A

Abbott, Deborah, *62*
Abbott, Harris, *60*, 77–78, 125–26, 132
Abbott, Jan, *60*, 77–78
Abbott, Tom, *136*
Abraham, Mount, 9, 17, 56–57, 103; alpine meadow, 159, 163; hikers on, *35*, *98*; ownership, 163; in winter, *144*
Act 250, 55
adopter program, 60, 135, 138–39, 179
Aiken, George D., 50, 55
Aldie Gannett Long Trail Stewardship Fund, 176
Allis, J. Ashton, 43
alpine meadows, 82, 85, *159–63*; on Camel's Hump, 113, *159*; on Mount Mansfield, 17, *111*, 113, 117, 120, 159–60, 161; protection of, 61, 117
amphibians, 153–54
Antos-Ketcham, Pete, 176
Appalachian Mountain Club, 32, 34, 38
Appalachian Trail, 9, 29, 166; relocation, 137; shares Long Trail, 17, 98–100; trail adopter, 139
Ascutney, Mount, 31
Ascutney Mountain Association, 30
Atlas Tract, 174
ATVs, 176
Austin Brook, *15*

B

Babcock Trail, 175
Babcock Trail Extension, 179
backcountry ethics, 59, 61, 83–85, 117, 128. *See also* carry in, carry out; Leave No Trace
Baker Peak, *184*, *185*
Bamforth Ridge, 106
Bamforth Ridge Shelter, 24–25, 136
Barber, Rodney A., 60
Barclay, Glen, 126
Barrows Camp, *59*, 124, 134
Barstow Charitable Trust, 179
Barstow Foundation, 179
Battell, Joseph, 17
Battell Shelter, 127
Battell Trail, 103
bears, *152*, *155*, 156, 178
Beaver Meadow Lodge, 134
beetles, 162
Belvidere Mountain, 92, *122*, *167*, 170
Bennington Section, *36*, 38, 48
Big Basin Forest, 178
Big Branch Shelter, 135
Big Jay Tract, 174, *178*
Big Muddy Pond, *175*
birds, 156; Bicknell's thrush, 142, 152, *157*–58, 162, 178, 179; hermit thrush, 106; on Mount Mansfield, 162; ovenbird, *156*; raven, *174*; ruffed grouse, *155*, 156
Black Falls Tract, 178–79
black flies, 153
blazing. *See* trail work
blueberries, *146*
board of directors, GMC, 33
bobcats, 154, *155*
Bolton, Vt., *28*, 38
Bolton Lodge, *71*, 84, 118
Bolton Mountain, *48*, 179
Bolton Valley Holiday Resort, 179
Bomarc transmitter, 55
Bonney, Thelma, 93
boots. *See* footwear
Boy Scouts of America, 137
Boyce Shelter, 105
Brandon Section, 38
Bread Loaf Section, 38
Breadloaf Wilderness, *15*, 132
bridges. *See* Clarendon Gorge bridge; Lamoille River bridge
Bristow, Preston J., 62, 166
Bromley Mountain, 138
Bromley Shelter, 137
Brownell, C. W., 33
Bruce Peak, 49
Bryant Camp, 84
Bryce, James, 32, 34
Buchanan, Andy, 49
Buchanan, Bruce, 45, 49
Buchanan, Chet, 49, 127
Buchanan, Helen, 124
Buchanan, Roy O., *45*, *49*, *124*, 123–25, 127, 131, 136
Buchanan Lodge, *134*
Buchanan Mountain, 49
Buchanan Shelter, 179
Burdick, Leah, *137*
Burke, Mountain, 31, 55
Burlington, Vt., 32
Burlington Section: Butler Lodge hikes, 83–84; and caretaker program, 114; death of Judge Cowles, 38; James Taylor resolution, 53; and 1938 hurricane, 49; oyster stew hikes, 77–78; at Taylor Lodge, *35*; trail builders, 134; trail maintainers, 136
Burnt Rock Mountain, 18, *176–77*, 178
Burr and Burton Academy, 137–38
Burt, Craig O., 36, 38
Butler Lodge: built by Buchanan, 124–25; Burlington Section hikes to, 83–84; caretakers at, 114, 120–*21*; night at, *108*; rebuilding of, *130*
butterflies, 141, *153*, *155*, 162
Buzzell, George, 179

C

Camel's Hump, 17–18, 86; alpine meadow, *159*, 163; in fall, *186–87*; formation of, 146; hikers on, *11*, *31*, *68*, *101*; Long Trail on, 19; ranger-naturalists on, 60; south knob, 25; spring hiking ban, 59; state-owned, 163; summit caretakers, 109–13, 114, *117*, *119*, 163; Wind Gap, view from, *41*; in winter, *54*, *80–81*, *107*
Camel's Hump Club, 30, 38
campfires, 74, 83, 85
camps. See overnight sites
Canadian border, *45*
caretaker program, 24, 109–19, *120–21*; caretaker at Barrows Camp, 59; and hiking boom, 22, 59–60; summit caretakers, 94, 106, 163; and trail work, *114*. *See also* Ranger-Naturalist Program
Carleton, Phillips D., *45*
Carmel Camp, 53
carry in, carry out, 59, 83
Catamount Trail, 29, 173, 179
Catamount Trail Association, 179
Cave Dog, 95–96, 105
Chamberlain, Allen, 44
Champlain, Samuel de, 32
children, *60*, 92, *93*, *100*, *104*, 135
Chittenden County Uplands Conservation Project, 179
Christiansen, Scott, 133
Civilian Conservation Corps, 50, 132
Clarendon Gorge, 53, *99*
Clarendon Gorge bridge, 23, *97*
Clarendon Lookout, *102*
Clark, Bill, 24
Clayton, Erna, 93
Cliff Trail, 133
climate change, 163, 181
clothing: modern, 87; post–World War II, 76–77; pre–World War II, 68, 70–72, 74, 90
Coffin, R. L., *74*
Cold War, 55
Congdon, Herbert Wheaton, *48*, 72
cooking, *36*, *40*, *73*, *82*, *90*, *121*. *See also* provisions; stoves
Cooley Glen, *36*
Cooley Glen Lodge, 53
Cooper, Charles P., 44
Cooper Lodge, 125
corridor monitoring. *See* stewardship program
Couching Lion Farm, 48
Cowles, Clarence P.: death of, 38; and Green Mountain Parkway, 50; trail builder, 36–38, 43, 44; winter enthusiast, 71–72; on women members, 59
Cowles, Laura, 59
Cowles Cove Shelter, 178
Cummings, Charles R., 38
Curtis, Jane, 38
Curtis, Will, 38

D

Davis, Deane C., 55
Dean, Howard, 166, *169*
Dean, Theron S., 43, 44, 67–71
Dean's Cave, 71
Dean's Panorama, *37*
DeBoer, Joseph A., 32
Deer Leap Mountain, *85*
Depression. *See* Great Depression
Derby Elementary School, 62
development pressures. *See* economic development pressures
Devil's Gulch, *143*
Dillingham, William P., 32
Dimock, Mark, 178
Doll, Charles G., *45*
Donovan, Al, *113*
Dove, Nan, *59*
drinking water, *20*, 87, 118
Dufresne Job, *73*
Dunsmore Lodge, 48

E

easement violation, 174–76, 183–84
economic development pressures, 182; in future, 183, 184; landownership, changes in, 22, 166; in northern Vermont, 62, 166; from ski areas, 55. *See also* Green Mountain Parkway; ski areas

education program, 22, 24, 61, *101*. *See also* caretaker program
Edwards, Smith, 77
Eich, Cat, 174
Elmore, Mount, *100*
Emily Proctor Shelter, *90*, 125, 132
Emily Proctor Trail, 132
end-to-end hikers: as authors, 88, 105; as fund-raisers, 62, 170; Governor Dean, *169*; during hiking boom, 59; at intersectionals, 78; trail names of, 98–99; women, 72–75, 78, 90–93, 98–100, 106. *See also* speed records
environmental conservation, 61, 172–73. *See also* Act 250
Equinox, Mount, 31
equipment: modern, 83, 87; post–World War II, 77; pre–World War II, 68, 72, 74
ethics. *See* backcountry ethics
Evans, Eric, *127*

F

farms, 44, 90–91, 182, 184
Fay Fuller Camp, 47
Fenn, Mary Beardsley, 92
Fiebig, Al, 131
Fields Pond Foundation, 179
fire patrol trail, 38–40, 42
fire towers, *26–27*, *48*, *115*, 135
fire wardens, 92
Fish, Bob, 135
Fish, Marge, 135, 137–38
Fisher, Dorothy Canfield, 47, 50, 103–5
fishers, 154
Fitzgerald, Brian, 172
Flanders, Ralph, 50, 55
flood, 1927, 48
flowers: clintonia, *173*; diapensia, 160; fireweed, *8*, *22*; red trillium, *149*; three-toothed cinquefoil, *162*; trout lily, *151*. *See also* alpine meadows
food. *See* provisions
footwear, *23*, 70–71, 77, 87
Forehead Bypass, *121*
French Camp, 134
fund-raising. *See* Long Trail Protection Campaign

G

Gannett, Aldie, 169, 176
Gannett, Robert T., 62–64, 169
geology, 142–46
giardia, 87
glaciers, 145–46, 162–63; pothole, 178
Glastenbury Mountain, 14
Glen Ellen Lodge, 105
Glen Ellen Shelter, *69*
Goodridge, Basil, *134*
Governor Clement Shelter, 23
Grant, Mount, 141–42, 158
Grauman, Muriel, 92
Great Depression, 50, 52, 182
Greater Vermont Association, 40
Green, Ned, 105
Green Mountain Club (GMC): as agent of change, 13–14; antiauthoritarian, 24–25; completion of Long Trail celebration, 47; decline, periods of, 40, 52; as environmental steward, 10, 14, 21, 22, 172–73; founding of, 9, 14, 21, 32–33; future of, 184; in Great Depression, 50–52; incorporation of, 61; mission of, 11, 14, 21–22, 30, 32, 64, 133; non-partisan, 26; in post–World War II era, 55; in World War I era, 40; in World War II era, 53. *See also* board of directors; Green Mountain Parkway; headquarters; membership; sections; staff; volunteers; names of programs, e.g., education program
Green Mountain National Forest, 29, *60*, 132, 166
Green Mountain Parkway, 21, 22, 50–52, 182
Green Mountains, 13, 14–21, 30. *See also* geology
Greszler, Kevin, *99*
Griffith Lake, 114
Griffith Lake Shelter, *40*
Griswold, J. Laurence, *73*
guidebooks, *24*, 44, 53, 60

H

habitats. *See* natural communities
Hagar Clearing, *36*
Haigh, Jean, 135
Hall, Violet May, 90, 92
handicapped-accessible trail, *128–29*
Hard, Walter, 50
Hardy, Dave, *126*, 129
Hare, Irving, *36*
Harmon Hill, *63*
Harrington, Jack, 49, 136
Harrison, Blake, 50–52
Haselton, Seneca, 33
Hawes, Austin F., 38
Hazen's Notch, *76*, *164*, 178
Hazen's Notch Camp, 53
Hazen's Notch State Forest, 178
Headquarters, GMC: in Montpelier, 61; in Rutland, 61; Waterbury Center campus, 49, 61, 124, 172
Hedgehog Brook Trail, 127
helicopter drops, 131–32
Hell Hollow Camp, *43*
hike-a-thon, 62, 170
hikers, 98; in alpine area, *82*; on Camel's Hump, *11*, *31*, *68*; in Clarendon Gorge, *97*, *99*; near Clarendon Lookout, *102*; near Clement Shelter, *103*; at Dean's Panorama, *37*; on Deer Leap Mountain, *85*; at Glen Ellen Shelter, *69*; at Lincoln Gap, *51*; on Lincoln Mountain, *33*; on Mount Abraham, *35*, *98*; on Mount Mansfield, *46*, *52*, *79*; in northern hardwood forest, *148*; preparing to climb, *69*; at Route 103, *84*; south of Burnt Rock Mountain, *176–77*; near Sterling Pond, *88*; near Stratton Mountain, *21*. *See also* end-to-end hikers
hiking boom, 1960–70s, 79, 83, 117; alpine meadows, effect on, 163; caretaker program expansion, 117; GMC reacts to, 59–61, 83; threat to Long Trail, 22; trail work expansion, 127–28
Hill, Don, 179
Hinchey, Minerva, *61*
hobblebush, *149*
Holden, Clem, 136
horsehair fungus, 142, 157–58
Houston, Dan, 170
Hump Brook Tenting Area, *104*, *137*
Hunger, Mount, 12, 31
Hunt, Leigh, *90*
hurricane, 1938, 49
huts. *See* overnight sites

I

Ingalls, E. L., 33
intersectionals, 59, 78–79
Ira Allen, Mount, 178

J

Jay Camp, 179
Jay Loop, 179
Jay Pass, 174
Jay Peaks, 17, 55, 87, *167*, *178*, 183–84
Johnson, Charles W., (sidebar) 159–63
Johnson, Joseph B., 55
Johnson, Vt., 48
Jones, Peggy, 92
Jonesville, Vt., 166
Joudry, Jeanne, *115*
Journey's End Camp, 49, *105*, 124, *172*, 179
Journey's End Trail, 172, 179

K

Kazarian, Nancy, 92
Killington Peak, 14–17, 31, 34, 55, 93, 114
Killington Section, 49, 59, 135
Klutznik, Katy, 95–96, 98–100, 103–5, 106
Koerber, Arthur B., 53, 55
Kurth, Hilda, 90–*91*
Kurtz, Jonas, *125*

L

ladders, 127
Lake Champlain Tercentennial, 32
Lake Pleiad Shelter, 53
Lamoille River bridge, 127, *129–31*
land acquisitions, 26, 62, 64, 116, 165, 178–79. *See also* Long Trail Protection Campaign; names of acquired tracts, e.g., Meltzer Tract
Lane, Gardiner, 136
Laura Woodward Shelter, *136*
Leach, Leo, 136
Leahy, Patrick, 116, 169
Leave No Trace, 61, 117, 184
Lenner, Robin, *120–21*
Lewis, Sinclair, 50
Lieberman, Frank, 38
Lincoln, Robert L., 62, 169, 170
Lincoln Gap, 9, *51*
Lincoln Mountain, 31, *33*, *116*
Line Post 592, *45*
Little, Leroy, 72
Little Rock Pond, 14, 91
Lockwood Pond, *170–71*
lodges. *See* overnight sites
logging, *173*
logo, *44*
Long Trail: Bill McKibben on, 10; building of, 14, 18, 36–45; *Burlington Free Press* on, 18–21; completion of, 45–46, 47; conceived on Stratton Mountain, 13, 32; future of, 181–84; hiker numbers, 22, 83, 182; Marion Urie on, 74–75; during World War II, 53, 76. *See also* easement violation; economic development pressures; guidebooks; hiking boom, 1960–1970s; Long Trail Protection Campaign; Monroe Skyline; overnight sites; publicity; entries under trail, e.g., trail signs
Long Trail Lodge, *47*, 52, 114

Long Trail News, *84*
Long Trail Patrol (LTP), 87, 123–32; dissolved during World War II, 53; founding of, 49; group of, *21*; and hiking boom, 59; volunteer LTP, 123; at work, *92*. *See also* Clarendon Gorge bridge; Lamoille River bridge; trucks
Long Trail Protection Campaign, 62–64, 165–66, 170–79; federal funding, 116; fund-raising projects, 62, 170; launching of, 62; Long Trail Protection Fund, 169; 265 Mile Club, 62, 170. *See also* land acquisitions; names of acquired tracts, e.g., Meltzer Tract
Long Trail State Forest, 165, 173
Lost Pond Shelter, 133

M

MacKaye, Benton, 9
McLaughlin, Walt, 88
Mad River Glen Ski Area, 55
Mansfield, Mount, 17; alpine meadows, 17, *111*, *120*, 159–60, *161*, *163*; caretakers on, *94*, *106*, *113*, 163; first winter ascent, 72; hikers on, *46*, *52*, *60*, *79*; preski trails, *51*; ranger-naturalists on, 60; road up, 31; ski area, 55; summit ownership, 163; summit ridge, *52*, *88–89*; survey taker, *62*; towers on, 55; Upper Lip, *142*; visitor numbers, 163
maps, 33, 34
Marasmius androsaceus, 142, 157–58
Martin, Hilda. *See* Kurth, Hilda
Massachusetts Institute of Technology, 68
Mathers, George, *43*
May Farm, 1836, 61
Mazza, Richard, 62–64, 169
measuring. *See* trail measuring
Meltzer Tract, *167*, 170, 171
membership, 24, 44, 59, 62, 64, 182
missile transmitter, 55
Monadnock, Mount, 135
Monroe, Will S., 42–44; and dogs, *42*, *44*; founder of New York Section, 43–44; hike leader, 71; his place names, 37, 71; at Long Trail Lodge celebration, 47; and 1927 flood, 48; preparing to climb, *69*; trail builder, *39*, *42*
Monroe Skyline, 17, 42–44, 178
Montclair Glen, 43, *64*
Montclair Glen Lodge, 109–13, 118
Montpelier, Vt., 61
Montpelier Section, 24–25, 77
Moore, Matt, 176
Moosalamoo, 9
moose, *156*, 174
Mould, Henry, 134
Mould Lodge, 134
Mount Mansfield Section. *See* Burlington Section
Mount Mansfield Summit House, 110
mushrooms. *See Marasmius androsaceus*
Musketeers Two, 170

N

National Register of Historic Places, 131
natural communities, 146–49; krummholz, 157; montane spruce–fir forest, 151; northern hardwood forest, *148*, 149–51
Nature Conservancy, The, 64, 170
Neubauer, Paul, *126*
New Deal, 50, 182
New York Section, 43–44, 48, 59
Norris, Kathleen, 90–*91*
North Branch School, 10
Northeast Kingdom Section, 135
Northrop, Robert P., 62, 170
Nuquist, Andrew S., 24–25, 26
Nurian, Kerson, 43

O

Okemo Mountain, 55
Open Space Conservancy, 179
Otis, David, 84
Ottauquechee River, 129
Ottauquechee Section, 137, 138–39
outhouses, 179; composting, 60, 110, *117*, *121*; humor, 83, *127*
overnight sites: built by Buchanan, 49, 124–25, 131; built by Tobiasons, 137; construction of, 24–25, *39*, *60*, *134*; crowding at, 87; farm lodgings, 44; rebuilding of, *87*; and woodstoves, 83, 110–13; work by Long Trail Patrol, 124–26, 131–32. *See also* names of sites, e.g., Taft Lodge
oyster stew hikes, 77–78

P

Page, Carroll S., 32
Paris, Louis J., 34, 40, 43, 44
Paris, Olden, 43, 44
Partridge, Alden, 30–31
Pearce, Paul, *125*
Pearlstein, George, 60
Peet, Harry T., 61, 62, 170
Pelsue, Lucile, 72–75, 91
Peru Peak Shelter, 132, 135
photography, 67–71
Pico Camp, 125,
Pico Peak, 52, 55, *85*
Pisgah, Mount, 31
place names, 37, 71
Plymouth, Vt., 78
porcupines, 34, 72, *154*
Preston, Frederic, 61
privies. *See* outhouses
Proctor, Fletcher D., 32
Proctor, Mortimer R., 44, 47, 49
Profanity Trail, 126
promotion. *See* publicity
Prospect Rock (Manchester), 34
Prouty, George H., 32
provisions: mailing of, 90–91; modern, 83–84, 113; oyster stew, 77–78; post–World War II, 77, 114; pre–World War II, 72–73, 74, 114; stone soup, 78
publications program, 24
publicity, 38, 44, 68–71
Puffer, Louis B., 53, 71, 73, 75

R

Ranger-Naturalist Program, 60, 117. *See also* caretaker program
Rice, Emily, 84
Rice, Roderick, 83–84, *113*
Rice, Stephen, 61
Riendeau Tract, 64, 170
Ritterbush Camp, 124
Robbins, Catherine, 90–*91*
Robbins Mountain, 166
rodents, *154*, *155*
Rolston Rest Shelter, 131
romance, *31*, 84
Romance Mountain, *39*
Roosevelt, Franklin D., 50
Rose, Anya, *184*
Rose, Ben, 61, *184*; on Long Trail protection, 22, 176; on volunteer culture, 24–25; on woodstoves, 83
Rosenberg, Asa, *100*
Ross, Willis M., 44
Roundtop Shelter, 124, 179
Route 30, *74*
Route 58, 178
Route 100, 52
Route 103, *84*
Route 105, 174
Route 118, 179
Route 242, 174
Rutland, Vt., 61
Rutland Section, 38

S

Sanders, William, 134
sections, 32, 38, 134–35. *See also* intersectionals; names of sections, e.g., Montpelier Section
Shaffer, Dennis, 61
Shea, Susan, 64, 172, 174
Shear, Lexi, *104*
Shear, Linnaea, *104*
Sierra Club, 9
Simpson, Kimball, 169, 170
ski areas, 55, 87, 183
skiing, 52, 55. *See also* Catamount Trail
Skylight Pond Trail, 9
Skyline Lodge, 9
Smugglers' Notch, *147*
Snake Mountain, 31
snakes, 103, 154
Snow, Mount, 55
snowmobiles, 174
snowshoeing, *14*, *35*, *54*, *71–72*
Somerset Reservoir, 27
speed records, 95–96
spring hiking ban, 59
spruce-bough bedding, 83, 126, 128
staff, GMC, 24, 61, 62, 64, 134, 170
Stanhope Ridge, 178
Stark Mountains, 21
Sterling Pond, *88*
Sterling Section, 38, 134
stewardship program, 24, 174–76; corridor monitoring, 137, 168–69, 174, 176
Stori, Val, 109–19
Stotesbury, Lucy Butler, 178
stoves, 110–13; kerosene, 114; packable, *82*, 83, 85; wood, 83–84, 126
Stowe, Vt., *51*
Stratton Mountain, 14, 21; caretaker on, *115*; Long Trail conceived on, 13, 32; ski area, *55*; view from, *26–27*
Stratton Pond, 14, *16*, 20, 59
Stratton Pond Shelter, 137
Strong, Shirley, 55, *60*

Sucker Brook Lodge, 39
Sugarbush Valley Ski Area, 55
Sugarloaf Mountain, *164*, 178
Sullivan, Tim, *117*
surveys, *62*
Sutton Mountains, 174
Sweet Water Trust, 179

T

Taft, William Howard, 32
Taft Lodge, *115*; building of, 38; caretakers at, 59, 110, 113–14; interior, 75; woodstove, 126
Taylor, James P., *34*; conceives of Long Trail, 13, 32; death of, 53; founder of GMC, 32; and Green Mountain Parkway, 22, 50, 182; his map of Long Trail, *33*, 34; lodge dedicated to, *58*; at Long Trail Lodge, 47; Long Trail initiator, 34; no environmentalist, 21; president of GMC, 33; as promoter, 38; snowshoeing, *14*, *35*, 71; as trail builder, 36; withdraws from GMC, 40
Taylor Lodge, *35*, *58*, 77–78, 114
tenting, *36*, 39, *104*, 128
Thayer, Clark, *74*
Thayer, Paul W., 47
Theron Dean Shelter, *53*
Thompson, Rufus, *74*
Three Musketeers, 72, 75, 90–*91*, 170
Thundering Falls handicapped-accessible trail, *128*–29
Tillotson Camp, 124, 131, 170, 179
Tillotson Peak, 168
Tobiason, Erik, 135, 137
Tobiason, Laurel, 137
tourism, 30–31, 44, 55
towers, communication, 55, 166
trail fees, 182–83
trail magic, 100
trail measuring, *48*
trail names, 99
trail register, *63*
trail signs, *17*, *23*, *28*, *51*, *63*, *121*, 179
trail work, 24; blazing, 42; and hiking boom, 59; ladders, 127; Long Trail maintenance, 48–49; rock work, *38*, *105*, 122, *125*, *126*, 127–28; steel handholds, 133. *See also* adopter program; caretaker program; flood, 1927; hurricane, 1938
trail workers, *30*, *39*, *45*. *See also* Long Trail Patrol; volunteers
transportation, 30, 43, 53, 59, 181–82
trash, 83, 85
Trebitz, Heinz, 138–39
Trout River, 179
trucks: "Dakota," 128; "Joe," 128; Patrol Truck No. 1, 49, *124*, 128
Tye, Lula, 61

U

U.S. Land and Water Conservation Fund, 179
University of Vermont, 42, 49, 67, 163
Urie, Marion, *72*–75, 91

V

Van Meter, Larry, 61
Van Meter, Ralph, *74*
Van Ness House, 32
Vermont Academy, 34, 40
Vermont Bureau of Publicity, 38, 44
Vermont Chamber of Commerce, 40, 50, 182
Vermont Department of Forests, Parks, and Recreation, 59–60, 163, 173, 176
Vermont Division of Historic Preservation, 131
Vermont Environmental Board, 55
Vermont Forestry Department, 38, 43
Vermont General Assembly: allocations for Long Trail, 26, 62–64, 166, 169, 179; resolutions honoring GMC, 26, 59
Vermont Housing and Conservation Board, 170, 179
Vermonter, The (magazine), 38
Vogt, Ted (sidebar), *168*–69
volunteers, GMC, 179; as adopters, 60, 138–39; as corridor monitors, *168*–*69*, 174, 176; as Long Trail Patrol, 123; as office staff, *61*; as trail and shelter workers, 24–25, 133–37; youth as, 137–38
Vondell, John, *53*

W

Wagner Woodlands, 166
Walker, Bill, *77*
Wallace, George J., *157*
Walsh, Kelly, 129, 132
Wampahoofus Trail, *121*
Washburn, Doris, 77, 78, 92
Washer Farm, 124
water. *See* drinking water
Waterbury Center, Vt. *See* headquarters
Waterman, Guy, 30, 32, 59, 90
Waterman, Laura, 30, 32, 59, (sidebar) 90–93
Watkins, Agnes, 91
Webster Camp, 48
Western, Greg, 129–30
White, Willis, *36*
White Rock Mountain, *12*
White Rocks Cliff, 14
Whiteface Mountain, 154
Whiteface Shelter, 125
Whitman, Walt, 42
Whitney, Don, 137
Whitson, Peg, 118
wilderness areas, 132
wildlife, 152–56, 162, 174, 182. *See also* individual species, e.g., porcupines
Wiley, Helen, 90
Wiley Lodge, 38
Wilgus, William J., 50
William B. Douglas Shelter, 131
Wilson, Stanley C., 47, 50
Wind Gap, *41*, 118
Winooski River, 38, 48
winter outings. *See* oyster stew hikes; skiing; snowshoeing
women: end-to-end hikers, 72–75, 78, *90*–93, 98–100, 106; first GMC president, 55; GMC members, 59; outdoor clothing, 71, 72, 74; as trail workers, 39, *92*, *122*, 132, 137–38
Woodbury, Urban A., 32
World War I, 40–41
World War II, 53, 76
Worth Mountain, 105
Wren, Christopher, 100

Z

Zwick, Daan, 49, 110, *113*–14, 118

THE GREEN MOUNTAIN CLUB PRESIDENTS

James P. Taylor 1910–1916
Mortimer R. Proctor 1916–1917
C.P. Cooper 1917–1925
Mortimer R. Proctor 1926–1933
Herbert W. Congdon 1933
Wallace M. Fay 1934–1935
Louis B. Puffer 1935–1941
Waldo C. Holden 1941–1942
Walter S. Atwood 1942–1944
Laurence W. Dean 1944–1946
Theodore N. Goddard 1946–1949
Roy O. Buchanan 1949–1954
Craigue S. Perkins 1954–1956
Leone E. Smith 1956–1957
Harold C. Collins 1957
Art Koerber 1957–1959
Don Kent 1959–1961
John H. Vondell 1961–1962
Ben Rolston 1962–1964
Robert W. Humes 1964–1965
John H. Rohrbaugh 1965–1967
Robert W. Attenborough 1967–1969
Shirley J. Strong 1969–1971
George F. Pearlstein 1971–1973
John W. Nuffort 1973–1977
Ralph E. Bryant 1975–1977
Joseph E. Frank 1977–1979
Douglas A. James 1979–1981
James E. Wilkinson 1981–1983
Preston J. Bristow, Jr. 1983–1986
Joseph F. Cook 1986–1988
Brian T. Fitzgerald 1988–1991
Kimball T. Simpson 1991–1994
Paul W. Hannan 1994–1997
Rolf Anderson 1997–2000
Marty Lawthers 2000–2003
Andrew S. Nuquist 2003–2006
Richard Windish 2006–2009
Marge Fish 2009–

PHOTOGRAPHY CREDITS

Abbott, Harris: pages 54 (bottom), 60 (three photos: hut construction, summit group, children), 62.

Anderson, Tom: pages 2–3, 88–89, 186–87.

Applegate, Scot: pages 8, 87, 112, 115 (top), 117 (top), 125, 136, 167, 175.

Boisvert, Paul: page 55.

Blumenthal, Dave: pages 6 (map), 93, 100, 101, 102, 104, 146, 149 (top), 151 (top), 155 (bottom, right), 173 (left).

Cahoon, George: page 164.

Compos, Jamie: pages 22, 38, 63, 76, 105, 170–71, 173 (right), 183.

Faccio, Steven D.: page 154 (top).

Gardner, A. Blake: pages 12, 15, 41, 140, 150, 180, 185.

Green Mountain Club archives: pages 14, 21 (both photos), 24 (guidebooks), 33 (map), 34, 36 (left), 40, 42 (left), 43, 44, 45 (left), 47, 49, 51 (bottom), 52, 53, 58, 59, 61, 68, 69 (top), 71, 72, 73, 74, 75, 77, 84 (*Long Trail News* covers), 91, 124, 128, 157 (bottom).

GMC Burlington Section: pages 113, 134.

Hard, Stefan: pages 92, 114, 122, 126.

Houchens, Paul: page 54.

Karson, Jenn, page 148.

Kenna, Caleb: pages 23 (all photos), 84, 103.

Larson, Matt: pages 18 (right), 19, 65, 88, 119, 129, 142, 147, 153 (bottom), 155 (top left), 161, 162.

Leahy, Patrick J.: page 116.

Mohr, Brian (www.emberphoto.com): pages 66, 80–81, 82 (top), 144–45, 159.

Monkman, Jerry: page 143.

Morse, Susan C.: pages 152, 155 (bobcat), 156 (top).

Osborn, Elinor (www.agpix.com/osborn): pages 154 (bottom), 155 (top right).

Pellett, Alden: pages 10, 46, 86, 98, 102, 106, 108, 110–11, 115 (bottom), 117 (bottom), 118 (both photos), 120, 121 (all photos), 130, 131, 155 (bottom left), 174.

Pfeiffer, Bryan: pages 153 (top), 156 (bottom), 157 (top).

Riddell, Mike: page 169 (left).

Rose, Ben: page 184.

Shea, Susan: pages 132, 167, 168, 172, 177, 178.

Smith, Clyde: pages 60 (bottom left), 64, 78, 79.

Stori, Val: pages 133, 135, 158, 160.

Special Collections Department, UVM: pages 28, 30, 31, 32, 33 (hikers), 35 (both photos), 36 (top), 37, 39 (both photos), 42 (right), 45, 48 (both photos), 51 (top), 69 (bottom), 70.

Sullivan, Tim: page 137.

Wallace-Brodeur, Jeb: pages 16–17; 18 (left, top), 20, 25, 26–27, 85, 94, 99, 107, 163.

Wahl, Jonathan (Roughtumble photo): pages 90, 127 (top).

Zephyr, Patrick: pages 50, 56–57, 151 (bottom).